Turning on Your P.R.O.F.I.T.S Tap!

The 7 Secrets to Generating Revenue in your Business

Steve Jones

First published 2018
by Skills for Business Publications

© 2018 Steve Jones

The right of Steve Jones to be identified as authors of this work has been asserted by them in accordance with sections 77 and 78 of the Copyright, Designs and Patents Act 1988.

All rights reserved. No part of this book may be reprinted or reproduced or utilised in any form or by any electronic, mechanical, or other means, now known or hereafter invented, including photocopying and recording, or in any information storage or retrieval system, without permission in writing from the publishers.

ISBN: 978-0-244-39727-2

Typeset: Sylfaen

Printed and bound by Lulu

CONTACT
Email: steve@skillsforbusinesstraining.co.uk

Web: www.skillsforbusinesstraining.co.uk

DEDICATION

To my family and my partner Kim for their unswerving belief and support whilst writing this book and to all those who kept prompting me to write. Thank you.

Turning on Your Profits Tap | Steve Jones

CONTENTS

A Note on Resources — page 7

The Purpose of This Book — page 9

Introduction — page 11

Overview: Contextual Model — page 21

Purpose & Vision — page 30

Relevance — page 78

Outclass the Crowd — page 84

Find Your Client — page 113

Inspirational & Integrity-Driven Sales — page 128

Time Management & Capacity — page 155

Serve Your Clients — page 215

Conclusion — page 228

Turning on Your Profits Tap | Steve Jones

A NOTE ON RESOURCES

This is a practical book, full of practical exercises, worksheets and diagrams, to help you get a true understand of the principles I am teaching. As a result, to make it easier, all of the worksheets in this book are available full-sized and in colour as a free download from the following link:

https://www.skillsforbusinesstraining.co.uk/p/bookimages

Turning on Your Profits Tap | Steve Jones

THE PURPOSE OF THIS BOOK

In my experience of working with hundreds of business owners over the years, a business is only as successful as the belief of its owner. The purpose of this book is to challenge a business owner's thinking, so they can build or increase their current success.

I want to give potential and existing business owners a contextual way of thinking about their businesses so that they can make decisions fast, rather than be drawn into confusion and long winded thinking.

There are seven contextual steps to thinking about 'turning on your P.R.O.F.I.T.S tap outlined in this book. I've also added in how to 'dive deep' on each step, and created an action plan at the end.

I have outlined later in the book what contextual thinking is but here is a quick example:

Is what you are doing right now taking you further towards your goal or further away from it? If it is taking you further away, you now have the choice to stop and refocus.

You see in my experience there are two types of business owner: *the technician*, and *the owner.*

The 'technician' loves what they technically do and that's what they do. The 'owner', on the other hand, owns a business he or she loves.

Both have passion but both express it differently.

Let me give you an example using a printing company owner I worked with.

I asked him: are you a printer who offers printing services or are you a business owner who has a printing business?

The mindsets are entirely different.

This book is about creating that business owner mindset and a way of thinking that allows you to generate P.R.O.F.I.T.S. regardless of the size of the business.

Most businesses owners start a business because they are technically brilliant at something and have a passion for it. That's to be commended, but to run a business you need a different mindset. This book is about 'thinking differently' and creating that strategic mindset.

INTRODUCTION

Over the years, many people have asked me to write books. I've always shied away from it because I've either been too busy or didn't really feel I had anything to write about.

It started years ago when I was training coaches on behalf of Catalyst Training and a trainee coach called John Burley said to me: 'All your stories and all your anecdotes and all the stuff you taught us should be in a book.' And I said yes, but I don't really have the time, and I wasn't really interested. Next Ashley Lawrence, my friend from ABC Networks, tried to encourage me to write a book. It happened a third time when I did a presentation a few years back for the Euro Coach List and the organizer came up again and said: 'You should be writing a book about this stuff.' Well, I suppose up until now I'd convinced myself I was too busy, but now I've finally decided to write this book. It felt especially pertinent to do this since my good friend James Sale, owner of Motivational Maps Ltd, has written an article for the National Coaching Network around the model this book outlines, which I taught him some 12 years ago. He kindly attributes some of his amazing success to the model. I had still more encouragement when I was giving an overview of the model to a group of business owners local to me. Gavin Bain, the ex UK Franchise Owner for BNI, was in his own words 'blown away' with the model and insisted I tell him when the book was out. So I guess it's time to share and commit my thoughts on turning on the P.R.O.F.I.T.S./revenue tap and the seven secrets to generating revenue to paper.

But first a bit about me and why I might be qualified to share the knowledge.

My background is in health and fitness management. I was fortunate to be part of management team of Fitness First PLC, one of the fastest growth businesses ever in the UK, we went from one club on the South Coast to the largest independent health club chain in Europe, then the world, all within a 7 year period. We took the AIM and FTSE by storm and at one point were opening a club a week and 2 world-wide. It was breathtaking fun; we did a lot of things wrong, and we did a lot of things right, and it gave me first hand experience of being in a fast growth business at the sharp end.

I left Fitness First when it became too much of a corporate, which left me feeling like a bit of a square peg in a round hole. I just didn't fit into the corporate beast it had become. Once it became more about the stakeholders than the staff and clients, once the entrepreneurial spirit died, I simply didn't fit.

I left and I didn't do anything for about six months; I walked up and down the beach, with my Jack Russell in tow, looking a bit like a lost soul, wondering what I should do next.

It was at that point that I decided I could actually help a few businesses grow, based on my experience, so that's what I did. Within six months I was approached by an international coaching organization called Shirlaws Business Coaching, who were setting up in the UK. They had seen what I was up to and invited me to work with them.

Shirlaws were, and still are, an amazing Australian based company that specializes in coaching SME clients (small medium sized enterprises). I was the first person to join them in the UK, after their directorships.

It was fascinating, interesting, and great fun, because all the philosophies, all the techniques, all the tools they were teaching me, mirrored perfectly my Fitness First journey.

What I realized was I now had all the tools, techniques and frameworks to enable fast growth, plus the experience of being involved in a fast growth business.

Three years into my Shirlaws journey I decided that there was something still missing. If you look at any business, you'll quickly work out that 'Process runs Business and People run Process'. The bit that was missing in all of this for me was the 'People' piece.

I see companies grow and lose their talent in the process. I didn't want that to happen to companies that I worked with.

So I left Shirlaws and set up Skills for Business Ltd, I decided that I wanted to do both 'process' and 'people' because what I was beginning to realize about really successful businesses was this: In order to have a great business you need 'great processes' and 'great people' and what I was seeing all too often was businesses that had either great process and poor people or great people and poor process. In the SME world it's usually great people and poor process.

This first book, therefore, is about process, the process of generating revenue with good profit. Every business needs to survive and in order to survive you need to generate profit.

In this book I'm going to start looking at turning on your P.R.O.F.I.T.S. tap, or what I term 'the 7 secrets to generating revenue' model and this is what I taught James Sale all those years ago.

Once I've written this first book on process and generating revenue, I'm then going to turn my focus to writing how to recruit, train and retain great people by developing great leaders and how that creates great employee engagement, so there's my second and third books.

But for now, I want you to understand that actually having great processes is the key to generating revenue and that there is a 7 step process for generating revenue and turning on your P.R.O.F.I.T.S tap.

When I present on this subject, I usually get the audience to do a brief exercise and I'd like to do the same with you. I'd highly recommend you try it if you want to get the most out of reading this book.

I'd like you to make a list everything you need to do to generate revenue in your business. And by 'everything', I mean everything.

That's: phone calls, emails, collecting money, banking money, everything you need to do to generate revenue, not just working with clients or getting clients, but everything you think you need to do. Now, if you've done that you probably have a long list and I think there's probably about 180 things that could be on that list. Here are some examples:

I MEAN EVERYTHING...Things Like...

- Advertising
- Promotions
- Emails Campaigns
- Networking
- Social Media
- Presentations
- Books
- Sales meetings
- Referral Programmes

- Follow Up Calls
- Product Development
- Strategy
- Support Services
- Client Meetings
- Alliances
- Creating Your Poistion
- Vision
- Lead Generation
- And many more......

There are a myriad of things you could be doing. The challenge with this is quite simply to ask yourself one important question: did you start your business to do all of this or did you start your business to do what you love doing?

What I find with business owners is that they get quite overwhelmed when they look at the list they've written down.

The next question I might ask the room is: Do any of you employ staff? And a few hands may go up. Next I ask Do they have job descriptions? Usually the answer is 'Yes'. Then I turn to the list we've collected on the flipchart and I say: *This is now your job description! How does that make you feel?*

It's impossible to be responsible for all those things by yourself and grow a successful business.

So, this is what I call *content* in a business and it's all the content that gets in the way of you achieving your objectives. So how do we make sense of all this content? You need to create a *context* (a way of looking at all that content).Let me explain what I mean.

This book is about setting your context around generating P.R.O.F.I.T.S. All that stuff on your list is just content and it sits below the line in this diagram below – your business and all the things you need to do to generate P.R.O.F.I.T.S. However, if I give you 7 simple CONTEXTS to align it to, it will be very quick and easy for you to make decisions.

CONTEXT

RADIO	SPONSORSHIP	ADS
EMAIL	REFERRALS	MAIL
PHONE	PR	SEMINARS
NETWORKING	MARKETING	INTERNET/ONLINE

CONTENT

What do I really mean by that? This book is about creating a context that enables you to look at the content and make sense of it fast.

So let's take a simple example to explain what I mean.

CONTEXT

ORANGES APPLES

CONTENT

Two Fruits: oranges and apples. If we had to make a decision to take oranges or apples to market – and we have say 30 or 40 business owners in a room, how long would it take to get a unanimous decision?

Well, it's probably going to take an age and probably to get out of the room you're going to get brow beaten into an arbitrary decision between either oranges or apples.

Now let's say we choose oranges to take to market, just to get out of the room, and it fails, what do all the people who wanted apples say? 'I told you so'. Here, you've got no unity, and this is what I call *content discussion.*

Now let's apply a *context* to the situation in order to make a decision fast, that everyone agrees on.

So what's the context we're looking at to make a decision fast? Well if we put 'vitamin C' as the context, it's very quick and easy to see that it's oranges. If we now take oranges to market, win or lose, there's still unity in the business.

Equally, had the context to make a decision been 'roughage' we'd have chosen apples and if we then took apples to market, win or lose we will still have unity. So it is about setting a *context* to make decisions around *content* fast.

Context is how to strategically think about *content* so we can make correct decisions fast.

What I'm going to do with P.R.O.F.I.T.S. is to give you the same; I'm going to give you 7 CONTEXTS to generating P.R.O.F.I.T.S. and then back it up with the *content* (things that need to happen around the context)

So, there you have it.

The *content* is the list of 180 things you can do to generate revenue (your list from earlier). The 7 CONTEXTS I will show you will enable you to generate P.R.O.F.I.T.S. by making sense and decisions fast around of all that content.

So, we are now at that point where we can look at the contextual model I'm going to be working through with you in this book.

The Seven Steps to Generating Revenue Contextual Model

1.PURPOSE & VISION

The first thing you need in a business is a *vision*. Do you have a vision for your organization? What's it going to look like in 3 years time? What's your purpose? Why did you set it up? Where is it all going? What's it going to look like? How much money is it going to generate? If you could take yourself out 3 years, what would your business look like? So that's what I look for when we talk about the context of PURPOSE & VISION.

It was Harvard that said:

> *'Companies with an unusually clear vision outperform their competitors by a factor of 10'*

So the section on PURPOSE/VISION is all about what your business is going to look like, how much revenue and profit it is going to generate, what it's going to be doing, who your clients are, how many you will have etc. It is also going to look closely at why you started this particular business: Your Purpose.

So it all starts by getting clear on your PURPOSE & VISION.

2. RELEVANCE: Products and Services

The next thing to consider after you've got your PURPOSE & VISION clear is; do you have products and services that people want?

If we were selling typewriters in today's society, it would probably be very difficult unless we found a vintage market. There is a need to look at your products and services – are they in demand, are they needed?

These days it is not enough to have just one product and/or service people want, because you really want your clients coming back for more. Therefore, do you have more than one product? It is wise as a business to consider what additional products and services you might offer your existing clients to keep them engaged with the business.

3. OUTCLASS THE CROWD with your Positioning!

Now you have your PURPOSE & VISION mapped out, you know what products and/or services are RELEVANT and therefore likely to be in demand. The next thing to look at is how you are going to stand out in a crowded marketplace. How you are going to OUTCLASS THE CROWD by getting clear on your market position.

For me 'OUTCLASSING THE CROWD' by getting clear on your market position is the most important thing you can do. If you get nothing else from this book other than learning how to position yourself or your business then I will be able to sleep at night knowing a big part of my job will have been achieved.

So how do you OUTCLASS THE CROWD by getting clear on your market position?

If you think back to your school days, you can probably remember the school bully, the top sports person, and the classroom swat. They have all created a space in your mind around who they are and what they do. They probably will have done this unintentionally. Nevertheless, they have in effect created a position around who they are that has enabled them to stand out in your mind. Scarily people will create a position in their mind around who you are and what you do. Your job is to make sure that it is the right perception if you want to OUTCLASS THE CROWD.

Now consider this too: if you discovered a silver tray at a car boot sale, what would you pay for it? 50p - £5 possibly. Now, if that same tray were for sale in the high street – what price then? Possibly £20-£30. Now if that same tray was pride of place in Harrods – what price then?

You see it's not your product and/or service that determines value, it is the perception of your product and/or service which determines who will buy and at what price. I call this *positioning*.

So how do you position yourself in the market place? We'll be looking at this in a lot of detail later, because positioning is so very, very important. It is essential to know what your ideal market is, who you are selling to, at what price, plus the service levels you'll offer.

4. FINDING CLIENTS: Lead Generation

Now, if you've done these 3 things – PURPOSE & VISION, RELEVANCE, OUTCLASS THE CROWD by getting clear on your market position, that's great! But, you're still potentially the best kept secret!

The next *context* is FINDING CLIENTS: how do you generate leads? Now there's the difficult way: 10 phone calls, 3 appointments, 1 sale – or there's the method I like to teach which is 10 phone calls, 10 appointments, and 10 sales. What's more, *they'll* be calling *you,* not the other way around.

This is what I call *finding your supermarkets.* It's about forming strategic alliances. I'm going to talk in a lot more detail about how you create and manage those strategic alliances (supermarkets).

5.INSPIRATIONAL Sales

You now need to be an inspirational sales person.

If you've created a strong position in the market you are likely to be in front of your ideal clients. If you have not, you may be having lots of cups of tea with people who will never buy your service. You may not have your positioning clear or your strategic referrers(supermarkets) may not be set up right.

If, however, you've done your positioning correctly you'll be in meetings where people actually know what you do, how you do it, and what you charge almost before you walk in. You'll be in the right meeting because of your strong positioning statement and the efforts you put into lead generation and getting trusted partners (supermarkets) to refer you.

You now need a strategy to run an INSPIRATIONAL sales meeting. You need a sales meeting process.

In this section we'll look at whether you are pre-sold or not. The whole energy around the relationship of sales is going to be covered, leaving you with a sales process that enables you to convert meetings into new clients.

6. TIME MANAGEMENT: Capacity Planning and delivery of your service

If you've done your inspirational sales properly, you're going to have to manage your time, capacity and personal factory. In this chapter we'll explore how you manage your capacity and time. If you're a one-man-band for instance, how many hours have you got available to work with your clients versus running your business. Remember you only get paid a lot of the time when you're in front of your clients, with some exceptions.

So how do you run your personal capacity-time factory? If you're a business, how do you work out who does what and how do you become both effective and efficient in your organization? I'm going to be taking you through a whole program around getting efficient, both in terms of yourself, and your business.

This is so important and enables you to avoid being a busy fool. It is in fact so critical to success that it was one of the key workshops identified by Grant Thornton on their very successful Growth Accelerator Programme which I delivered for them. We called it 'More For Less'. I'll be taking you through the whole process. It will enable you to be super organized and efficient around your time.

7. SERVE: Delight Your Client

It is not just enough to just deliver your services these days, you have to delight your client, you have to excite them, you have to over-service them. So this section will be about making sure you do it in a way that generates energy around you and your business.

SUMMARY: A word about all seven points

Now if you do it well, one of two things will happen. Either they are going to come back and buy your second, third and fourth product, which is why I said you need more than one product, so you keep the client for life by bringing in new products and services they can buy.

Or, they will tell all their friends and their business associates what a great job you've done and become your greatest referral source.

If you've really done well, they might just do both.

Turning On Your P.R.O.F.I.T.S Tap

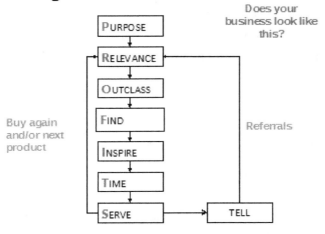

Now, look at the diagram above and imagine a tap at the top of the diagram which you can turn on. Instead of water, it's money that flows from the tap (wouldn't we all love one of those?). Provided that all these seven steps are in place, you can now see how the revenue will flow from top to bottom and recycle.

It's a bit like the fountains you find in gardens where the water cascades and recycles. As long as there are no blockages, the water will flow and the pump won't burn out.

If however, you have any blockages the water won't flow and eventually the pump will burn out.

Equally, if any of these seven steps are not functioning as they should, this will represent a blockage and restrict your profitability.

If there's a blockage, obviously your pump is going to break in the analogy of a fountain, so we need to make sure that all seven steps have a tick. So right now, I'm going to ask you to look at the diagram and put a:

√   if it is functioning

−   if it is working but not consistently

x   if it is not happening at all

In my experience, I find positioning is the key one where things are going wrong usually.

If you position your product wrong, you can end up in the sales meeting with the wrong type of client and as a result they will not buy your product or service resulting in your factory remaining empty.

How many sales managers have you seen sacked because they have been sent on a fool's errands, trying to make an impossible sale, because the company hasn't made its position clear?

If your factory, however, is full and your capacity is challenged, then you're usually very strong on position, possibly a victim of your own success.

The remainder of this book is going dive deep into the content of making the seven P.R.O.F.I.T.S. steps to generating revenue work for you.

If you follow these steps I know you'll have a great business experience. It works as well with start ups as it does with the most established businesses.

1. PURPOSE & VISION

'Companies with unusually clear visions outperform their competitors by a factor of ten' according to Harvard Business School.

This section is dedicated to looking at your three year vision by taking your business out three years.

- In this section we'll be looking at the nine areas of your business and showing you how to map them out on a canvas. This will enable you to explain your business to anyone in one simple diagram, be that a staff member or a client. It will also enable you to create a business where there is unity and helps avoid the silo mentality that can occur. It's also going to give you a lot of clarity around your business.

- We'll be looking at your purpose 'why' you do what you do and the importance of knowing your 'why'

- We'll be looking how you can create a visual representation of your vision that can be explained to the most senior or junior person in your business, as well as your clients, should you choose to do so.

I'll be asking questions like:

What business are you in? What will it look like in three years time? What is your purpose? Do you know your why?

Let's start by understanding your *why*.

What do I mean by your *why*? I want to bring your attention to the work of a gentleman called Simon Sinek and a TED Talk video entitled the Golden Circle. He wrote a book called 'Start With Why', where he outlines an intriguing theory.

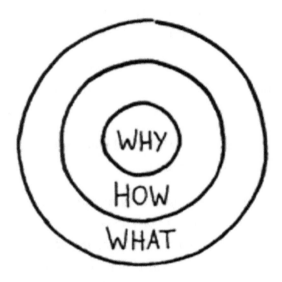

In his videos and his book he explains that those companies that are successful do the exact opposite to most other companies. He believes that most companies know 'what' they do, some know 'how' they do it, but very few companies know 'why' they do what they do.

He believes that it is the companies that start with and understand their 'why' who outperform their competitors.

He believes that people don't buy 'what' you do, they buy 'why' you do it.

To demonstrate what he means he uses 'Apple' and 'Dell' as an example, primarily because most people know of these two companies.

What he says is that they both, in essence, do the same thing. However, they are perceived differently.

He uses Apple to demonstrate how they hold true to their 'why', and what they would look like if they didn't.

'If Apple were like most other companies, a marketing message from them would move from the outside in of The Golden Circle. It would start with some statement of what the company does or makes, followed by how they think they are different or better than the competition, followed by some call to action. With that, the company would expect some behaviour in return, in this case a purchase. A marketing message from Apple, if they were like everyone else, might sound like this: 'We make great computers. They're beautifully designed, simple to use and user-friendly. Wanna buy one?'

Sinek contrasts this example by laying out how Apple actually markets themselves (or at least, how they used to):

'Let's look at that Apple example again and rewrite the example in the order Apple actually communicates. This time, the example starts with why: 'Everything we do, we believe in challenging the status quo. We believe in thinking differently. The way we challenge the status quo is by making our products beautifully designed, simple to use, and user-friendly. And we happen to make great computers. Wanna buy one?'

Apple as a company, 'We exist to challenge the status quo.' Apple has done this since their inception, challenging the idea of what a personal computer should be, what kind of expertise it should take to use one, and what the experience of the user should be like.

The reason he wrote this book was because he believed most companies get it wrong. His TEDTalk takes about 20 minutes to watch and will give you a sense of why you do what you do, and challenge you to understand your 'why'. Understanding why people *buy you* will be critical to your success. They can get your product anywhere, so why from you? We'll also be looking at this again in the positioning section.

I like to think people buy me because I help them think strategically. I help them think differently, I help them stay in context, manage their energy, and as a result shift and move. I like to think of myself as a game-changer, helping people become better at what they do: better leaders, better team leaders, better business owners, better

more engaging and profitable businesses. That's my 'why' to improve

and better people and businesses. Once you've worked out your why, I'd like to move you forward and begin to map your business out on a canvas.

Business Canvas Model

We're on to the second section of creating your vision now and the second section is to take that purpose, that 'why' and articulate it on a business canvas model adapted from the Business Model Generation, Osterwalder and Pigneur. Quite often you will need to be able to explain your business to your clients, to existing and any new staff that you take on. It also helps the bigger companies feel more holistic and less fragmented. There is a video on this to give you a brief overview, which you can find on YouTube by simply typing in: ' Business Model Generation, Osterwalder and Pigneur'.

There are apps for this business canvas model as well and you can even monetize it too in some instances.

For now, this is what the business canvas looks like and I'm going to get you to populate your own in this section.

The Business Model Canvas

Key Partners	Key Activities	Value Proposition	Customer Relationships	Customer Segments
What can partners do better or cheaper than us?	What are our key activities? How hard are they to copy?	Which one of our customers' problems / needs are we solving? Why us?	What relationships do customers expect?	For whom are we creating value by turning a need into demand? Who are our most important customers?
	Key Resources What are our key resources? How hard are they to copy?		**Channels** How will we reach our customer segments?	

Cost Structure		Revenue Streams	
What is the cost structure of our business?		What value are customers really willing to pay for? How will they pay for it?	

Adapted from Business Model Generation, Osterwalder & Pigneur

This is a visual model and it asks essentially nine questions:

1. Customer Segment: Who are your customers?

2. Value Proposition: What is your value proposition for each customer? What do you do for them?

3. Channels: How you find your customers? Your Channels to market

4. Customer Relationship: How do you interact with your clients?

5. Revenue Streams: How to you get paid for your bundles of product and services?

6. Key Resources: What key resources do you need to run your business?

7. Key Activities: What key activities do you need to do/perform in your business?

8. Cost Structure: What are your fixed and variable costs associated with running your business?

9. Key Partners: Which partners are essential to running your business?

Now look at this example and see if you can work out who this company is?

Turning on Your Profits Tap | Steve Jones

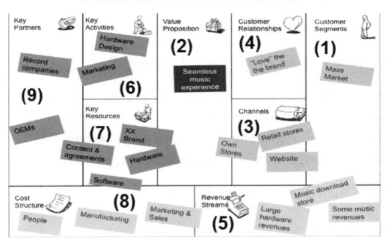

As you can see, it's very simple. This form allows you to distil an entire business down to the key elements. If you haven't guessed already, this Business Model Canvas is for the original Apple iPod.

So, if this is good enough for Apple to use, hopefully it'll be good enough for you to use for your business.

Let's get cracking! You'll need a copy of the blank canvas for this. I would recommend using an A0 size or as large as you can and populate it using post-it notes. If you have a team, get them all involved.

1. Customer Segments

Let's start with customer segments.

- For whom are you creating value?

- Who are your most important customers?

Let me talk about my business to give you an idea. My customers are business owners, entrepreneurs, teams, and companies that are looking to grow, (therefore I'm not really looking for lifestyle businesses, although my work may attract and apply to them).

Typically, Individuals and/or businesses:

- Who've got an entrepreneurial ideas

- Who are looking for coaching, mentoring and training

- Are prepared to invest their time and money

These are my customers.

Who are *your* customers?

Take a few moments to plot that out. Is it mass market, is it niche? I've got a customer whose business is specifically about looking after recent mothers returning to work, so that's a very niche market. A mass market proposition could be completely different. So who are your customers?

2. Value Proposition

Now you've identified those customers:

- What value do you deliver to them?

- Which one of those customers' problems do you solve?

- Which bundles of products and services are you offering to each customer?

- Which customer's needs are you satisfying?

In my business:

What I do is help individuals, teams and businesses think more strategically, so they can grow their people and their businesses fast.

My aim is to create stress free, highly profitable businesses, with great systems, where staff love being there, customers love being customers, and where the owner(s) can work *on*, not *in*, the business to continue its growth.

So my value proposition is coaching people and companies to improve performance, to shift, to think differently and to get better outcomes and results and to get more momentum. That's my value proposition. What's your value proposition? Again spend a few moments populating the box.

3. Channels

Once you've worked out your customers, worked out your value proposition, the very next thing is: how do you find your clients?

- Through which channels do our customer segments want to be reached?

- How do you find your clients?

(for me it's via strategic alliances; talks; presentations and referrals)

- Through which channels so your customer segments want to be reached?

(via presentations; recommendation; trusted partners)

- How are you going to reach them?

(by building strategic alliances; website; social media; referrals; presentations and talks)

- How are your channels integrated?

(Strategic Alliances lead to talks, to referrals, to meetings)

- Which ones work best?

(Strategic Alliances; Talks and Presentations; Referrals)

- Which ones are most cost efficient?

(Strategic Alliances; Talks and Presentations; Referrals)

- How are you integrating them with customer routines?

(Strategic Alliances; Talks and Presentations; Referrals)

I've identified my strategies in brackets underneath the questions. The way I get customers in through referrals and trusted partners, I work on building relationships with accountants, lawyers, IT companies who work with the clients that I want but don't do what I do. There is a whole section later in this book dedicated to how to do this and build these relationships, but in essence, when these strategic partners are with their clients and they start talking about growth issues in their business or being stuck, they can refer me. It's a great way to get business and we'll talk about that further. The other way is through public speaking engagements and through referrals from existing clients. I very rarely do cold calling. That's how I find my clients. Obviously I've got my website and social media too.

How do you find your clients? How do your clients find you? How are you creating awareness? How are you evaluating whether they are the right people? How easily can they buy your services?

Have a good think about your channels to market and fill in the box with your ideas. You'll be pleased to know that we'll be covering this again in more detail later in the book. So if you are not sure about how to find clients right now it will be covered again and in more depth.

4. Customer Relationships

- What type of relationship does each of your customer segments expect you to establish and maintain with them?

(very personal coaching & training with individuals, teams and businesses; key strategic relationships with trusted partners who refer me)

- Which ones have you established?

(strategic alliances and client relationships)

- How are they integrated with the rest of your business model?

(part of my overall strategy)

- How costly are they?

(inexpensive as they only require my time)

Once again, the examples in brackets are mine. My customer relationships in my business revolve around one-to-one relationships where I do individual coaching; I coach teams, I coach businesses. I work with tools like this. I do online work like this as well.

My relationship is one-to-one and is very personal, it can also be one-to-many, or it can be just through an online courses, but I'm very clear how I work.

I'm very clear on the relationship I want with my clients, because not only do I want to serve them well, I also want my clients to buy more services and to refer me. It's important I build trust in my business. Therefore, it is vital I build very strong relationships whenever I can.

What are your customer relationships like?

It doesn't have to be the same as mine. For instance, if we look at Amazon, Amazon do not have a one-to-one relationship with anybody, but they run a very efficient service. Apple's relationship is one where their intent is to love their clients to bits and they provide as much support as they can to their clients.

Therefore, choosing your type of relationship is quite critical. Spend a few moments identifying yours and make some notes in the box.

The next thing is revenue streams. You're doing all this stuff with good intent but you are in business to create value and get paid accordingly.

5. Revenue Streams

- For what value are your customers really willing to pay?

(business improvement; more time; more money; less stress)

- What things are they really buying?

(the ability to improve themselves, their people and their businesses)

- For what do they currently pay?

(Coaching; Training; Mentoring)

- How are they currently paying?

(via invoices; by retainer; per course; per session – but mostly programmes and retainers)

- How would they prefer to pay?

(some prefer to pay as they go per course; others like a retainer)

- How much does each revenue stream contribute to the overall revenue?

(split between my Employee Engagement Programme; Engaging Leaders Programme; Business Growth Coaching Service; Motivational Maps Training & Coaching; Licensing of Trainers/HR Professionals in my products)

I also have this book/online course. I make revenue through my book/online courses, I make revenue through my one-to-one working with individual coaching. I make money through working with companies and retainers with companies – they pay me a monthly retainer to go in and work with them. These are all my revenue streams and different ways that people can pay me.

So what are yours? How do you get your revenue? Is it one off payments? Is it recurring income? Is it a retainer? Is it charged by the hour? How do you get your revenue?

6. Key Resources

- What are the key resources that you need to run your business?

- What key resources do you need in place to run your business and service your:

- Values proposition?

(To maintain my value proposition I have several licensed products I need to ensure are maintained)

- Distribution channels?

(I rely heavily of strategic alliances with accountants, lawyers, IT Companies. I therefore need to manage my resources around maintaining these).

- Customer relationships?

(I have a number of regular clients that I need to maintain good relationships with, plus my strategic alliances, who I consider customers too)

- Revenue streams?

This could be physical, intellectual – which might be brand, patent, copyright – human and financial.

(My revenue streams rely on me updating my knowledge, my IP, and my licenses).

- IT System and Social Media structure

- Trade Association and Key Networking Memberships

If you take my business: I need an office. I need a laptop. I need a phone. I need support packages from Motivational Maps Ltd which I use, and other licensed products I use. I need the support of the bank manager. I need the support of my accountant. I need my social media person. So there's a whole range of key resources that I need to run my business effectively.

So what are the key resources you need and what are the costs of those key resources?

7. Key Activities

- What activities do you undertake on a daily basis?

- What key activities do your value proposition require?

(for me to attend and deliver what we have agreed in a timely fashion for the price agreed)

- Your distribution channels?

(For me to update them on any clients of theirs I am working with and to regularly meet to maintain the relationship)

- Your customer relationships?

(this can be wide reaching and include bank managers; suppliers; joint ventures; partnerships; as well as my existing clients)

- Your revenue streams?

(To maintain my revenue stream requires for me to deliver on my promise; invoice; collect money due; run my accounts. This requires regular meetings with my bookkeeper and accountant)

Let's give you an example from my business again. My key activities are constant social media to create awareness of my courses and availability, developing my one-to-one relationships, preparing the slides, the workshops, driving, delivering the workshops, my time involved in all of that, following up after the sessions, meeting new clients, signing up new clients, managing new clients. Designing new strategies and designing new workshops. These are all activities that I need to undertake, activities that, if left undone, would cause my business to fall apart, and my customers would no longer buy from me.

What are your key activities, the things you do your business can't do without? Take a moment and populate the box.

8. Cost Structure

All of these things cost money. Every business has overheads and costs.

- What are the most important costs inherent in your business model?

(I have licensing fees for products; equipment costs; office space; phone lines and mobiles; VAT, Tax and Bank Charges; Suits; Dry Cleaning; Petrol; Marker Pens; Computers; Flip Charts Etc. They fit into fixed and variable costs but they are all essential to running my business).

- Which key resources are most expensive?

(Licensing Fees are my biggest expense after my car and petrol)

- Which key activities are most expensive?

(Promotional Talks and Presentations; Networking; Travel; Client Sales Meetings – all of which are essential but for which no payment is often received)

So again, looking at my business, what's the cost structure to my business? There's fixed cost and there's variable cost. Fixed costs are things like my office. I have to pay for my website to be up all the time. I have to pay for my social media. I have to pay for quite a lot of things and those are my fixed costs. My variable costs could be the ink to print documents, travel, heating, lighting. Some things you buy in bulk you can get economies of scale on too, so think about what your cost structures are. What things do you have to pay for in order to run your business? Which ones are the most expensive and are there ways of saving money?

9. Key Partners

I couldn't run my business without key partners, so it's important to take a moment to identify just who they are and commit it to paper. I'm asking you to write a lot of things down, but sometimes it's only in the act of writing that things become clear. Fiction authors often admit that they do not know where their stories are going until they start writing them. Directing the narrative of your business is no different!

- Who are your key partners?

(My key partners are: the bank; website hosts; social media support; licensed product suppliers; accountant; key strategic alliances; trade associations etc)

- Who are our key suppliers?

(again all my strategic alliances that refer me business; licensed product suppliers; web hosting company; the bank; social media support; my accountant and bookkeeper)

- Which resources are you acquiring from your partners?

(I acquire business leads and clients; web platforms; licensed products; social media support; bookkeeping and accounts)

- Which key activities do partners perform?

(Bookkeeping and Accounts; social media; licensed products and opportunities to present to their clients and receive referrals)

I have a product called Motivational Maps I need to keep up-to-date with, paying on a monthly basis for the license in order to deliver that tool to my clients. That's one key partner. I have a similar set of tools I use in my 'Engaging Leaders Programme', for which I also pay a monthly license fee. These are the most obvious examples.

However, here are some you may not have immediately thought of: your bank manager; your bank manager is undoubtedly a key partner. Without their support, you probably wouldn't be able to run your business. Think too about your key suppliers – where do you get your equipment from? Where do you get the stationary you need?

A key supplier could also be your IT company. Without the IT support you wouldn't have a website, you wouldn't have social media, or may not even have any kind of infrastructure (depending on how key IT is to your business) so these are key partners and without them you may not be able to run your business.

It is really important to be aware of all of these partners and aware of any risk associated with losing their support.

If, for example, you used an IT person that was a one man band – and there's nothing wrong with that by the way – what would happen if they went out of business? Would you be exposed?

You need to be thinking about your key partners, about how safe those partnerships are and how vulnerable you are if things go wrong for them, or they change hands, or they become unable to deliver your service.

For me, where I use licensed products, I have to ask the question will the rules change? Will the pricing change? I need to know and therefore keep close relationships with both my key suppliers as well as my web-hosting company.

It is the same with my accountant, as I don't want any undue surprises due to taxation changes nobody has told me about.

We've now covered all the nine areas. Congratulations! Now you can take the model below and populate it, or you can download one of the apps on your iPad if you have one.

If you have a team, I recommend doing this on an A0 size sheet with post-it notes before recording it, so everyone can get involved.

The value of this model is that if anybody ever joins your business, you can immediately explain your business in one simple diagram. You can include it in your induction programme. Your receptionist can explain this to a new member of staff or somebody sitting in reception waiting to do business with you, should you choose.

They can see, crystal clearly, your whole business model if you want them to.

As I previously said, this model is brilliant for creating a united approach to business which negates any silo mentality which tends to creep in as businesses grow. I recently ran a session with a client and it really helped the whole team understand areas of the business outside of their own. This enables them to take more ownership of their role and what it contributes to the whole. There were some real 'aha' moments as team members from different areas gained huge insights into the 'bigger' picture.

It's also a fabulous tool if you've got a new activity or new project you want to map out too.

You can run this model with a new project just as well as with the an existing business, large or small. It works with the most experienced people in business as well as the most junior members. It's a great starting point and really makes you focus on your business.

By doing this you should get a real sense of purpose.

Setting Your 3 Year Vision

Hopefully by now you will have a real sense of why you do what you do and the nine key areas of your business. It's time now to look at the bigger picture and what your business will look like in 3 years time.

To do this, I'm going to use a visioning tool I called Vision Maximiser. When I do this with my clients I get as many of the senior management team together as possible so that it is a team effort that all contribute to and buy into.

Turning on Your Profits Tap | Steve Jones

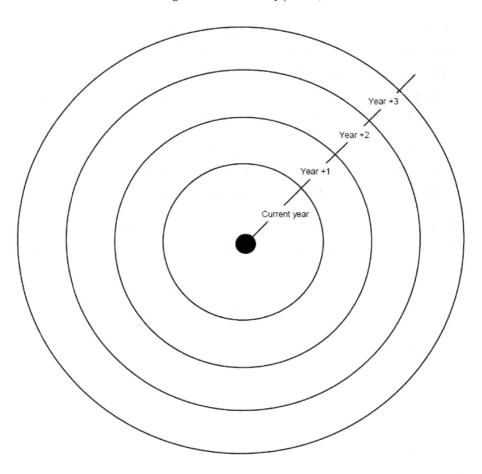

If it is just yourself, a single operator, it will still be as powerful.

To create the effect I want I typically use an A0 diagram poster which I spread out over a large table. You can use A3 or A4 if you prefer. Whilst this is typically "the next three years", the actual dates can vary slightly depending whether the company wishes to include their current financial year or begin the Vision at the start of next financial year. The choice is again yours.

Once the timeline has been agreed, the years can then be written inside the concentric circles working outwards as the time progresses with the latest date in the outside circle.

Next it is important to agree the measures of performance that would be most meaningful to you in describing the next three years. These become the axis labels around the outside of the Vision Maximiser diagram. They will typically but not exclusively include strategic growth measures or activities like:

- Sales Turnover
- Profit
- Number of employees
- New office locations
- New product launches on stream
- Changing % blend of customer types
- Amount or % of turnover from overseas
- Amount of turnover or % of turnover from adjacent markets
- Key strategic appointments to the team

- Raising finance
- Alliances/Strategic partners
- Acquisitions
- Quality standards/Accreditations

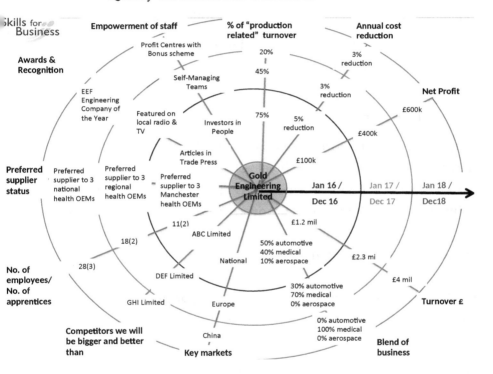

Starting with the latest year in the outer ring, I work with the team to insert the relevant numbers or descriptions around each of the 3rd year axis. By defining the 3rd year first, you can then work backwards from the future towards previous year's targets, thereby improving the chances of success.

Once you have completed your outer 3rd year ring, work each performance axis inwards individually. To do this you'll need to challenge yourself by asking yourself the following questions:

- If I were able to achieve this level of performance in year 3, what level should I be achieving in year 2?

- If that's my/our target for year 2, what's the minimum level of performance next year?

In this way, each performance axis can be allocated a number or a statement to indicate the level of performance. When I'm working with individuals and/or teams I find a good starting point is usually Profit and Turnover. It always amazes me how once this is agreed how it drives the thoughts on the other areas of the model so they fall into place.

In this way, you immediately get the opportunity to think of, discuss and define in clear terms how much growth is desirable and feasible.

Once you've agreed and completed the Turnover and Profit figure axis for all three years, it is then appropriate to consider some of the other axis labels to define and explain how you can realistically deliver this financial growth.

As I said I'm always amazed how this changes the way an individual or team looks at their business. It becomes a focusing point that facilitates ideas, and even better, action, like breaking into "new markets", "securing finance" even "key appointments" and "staffing levels". In essence, the visioning of your business should contain all the necessary high level information to tell you your businesses 3 year "growth strategy"

It should be noted that on occasions I have found that some individuals or businesses need to plot where they are first and gain value from plotting this current year's performance on the innermost ring to give some recognition of the stretch they are envisaging.

When the entire visioning diagram has been completed, which may possibly involve adding or subtracting new Axis labels, please take time to review the finished article with the team (or someone you know well if you work on your own).

Is it balanced and focused enough?

Do the numbers really stack up and relate to each other?

Year by year, is it easy to see how the strategy unfolds?

In which area is it most likely to experience problems?

Can anything else be added to help overcome any obvious gaps in logic?

Here is an example of a vision maximiser diagram from outset to completion.

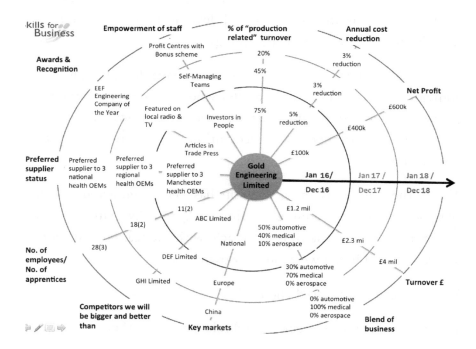

What does good look like?

Is the completed draft vision maximiser diagram you have in front of you sufficiently stretching across all relevant measures, especially if you want your business to be a high growth company?

In your mind, are there sufficient resources built into this Vision to help convert your strategic intent into operational activity? You should look particularly closely at the finding, winning, and growing customers processes?

If I were coaching you, I'd also be looking for any specific figures/statements that look odd or have been left unchallenged.

Is there a good mix of hard numerical business measures plus milestones or events, which help tell the story of the company's progress? It's not just about turnover!

Don't be afraid to bring it to life a little by including your own colours, images and key personal milestones to personalise the vision maximiser diagram; this will give it more meaning for you and your staff/team.

Well thought out visions like this create a sense of purpose for you and everyone else involved in the business.

If done correctly, they bind people together and provide momentum for change.

The true benefits of a vision maximiser diagram, however, only come when it is shared and understood by all stakeholders in a business including management, employees and even, key customers.

All need to understand what their contribution is and what they will gain personally from its successful accomplishment.

Finally the 'acid' test

This is not just a synonym for KPIs. This is something unique and different. It should be exciting to you, for a start, and be very visual. If it excites you, you are more likely to show the necessary passion to make it succeed.

Ask yourself, what do you want to be famous for? Does it express your purpose and passion? This isn't just business as usual.

Remember your 'why' and get motivated and excited by it. Use inspirational phrases as well as numbers. Get a clear sense of strategic direction and leadership. You are going places and you are taking the troops with you!

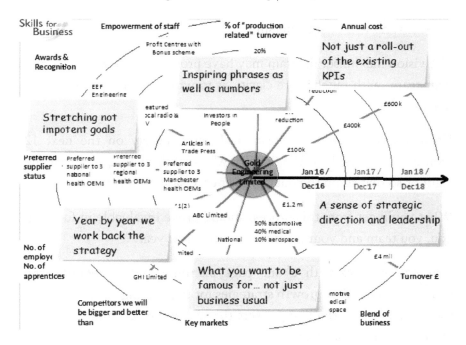

Single Page "One Year Sprint"

Even if you have a business plan, I have found it so useful to create a one page "One Year Sprint" that really focuses upon the year ahead, in particular:

- What the year ahead will look like
- How it will be achieved
- When it will be achieved

- Who will take ownership

The vision maximiser diagram may have provided you, the leader and your team, with much more clarity as to what the business will look like over the next 3 years.

However, this One Year Sprint is focused purely on the next 12 months. It helps distil the "vital few" breakthrough goals from the eight or so that sit on the outside of your Vision poster.

What you'll get from this process should prove invaluable in focusing you, you team and your business over the next year.

You will end up with a one page planning matrix detailing the company's Vital Few growth strategies for the coming year (known as the "Whats") plus the key projects that drive the accomplishment of these (known as the "Hows").

However, if you are a more established business, to maximise the value from the technique and to optimise buy-in, it is recommended to include the company's top management team at the very least.

The significance of this exercise is that high growth does not come easy; it does not just happen by adopting a "business as usual" approach. To achieve it, companies need to agree and action major strategic plans. Small improvements in performance or mediocre strategic steps will just sentence the company to another few years of average growth, drift, or worse.

What do you believe your company's "vital few" breakthroughs should be for the coming year? As the name suggests, these are the small number of critical strategic breakthroughs the company must achieve if it is to stay on target to achieve its Vision. You see, if you took all 8-10 strategies from your visioning diagram it would be too much to focus on and likely lead to a feeling of being overwhelmed, and a sense of failure, because no one can meet all those targets. However, if you pick 3 to 4, the ones I call the 'vital' few, to focus on for the coming year, the chances of dynamic growth and success are greatly increased.

Skills for
Business

TRADITIONAL THINKING:

*We can accomplish 8-10 large
strategic goals with excellence*

FAST GROWTH THINKING:

*We can only accomplish a maximum of 3-4 high
growth goals at once in a year with excellence.*

Consider these the 20% of actions that drive 80% of the outcomes of the Vision for that Year.

		Single Page Plan for:											
			SUPPORTING HOWS	P1	P2	P3	P4	P5	P6	P7	P8	P9	P10
			By Whom										
VITAL FEW	VF1												
	VF2												
	VF3												
	VF4												
		* Completely Relevant	Measure										
		O Contributes	Target (by when)										
		Leave blank if doesn't contribute	Performance										

Notes on Performance
Green — Going to plan
Amber — Needs some attention
Red — Not going to plan. Project might not be completed in time

In selecting the optimum Vital Few, ensure that you are only considering genuine breakthroughs and not just goals that would naturally occur anyway. Remember we are looking to achieve growth and profit, so the Vital Few Breakthroughs must represent a real stretch.

These Vital Few must be clear, compelling and easy to grasp. Ideally they are encapsulated in a fairly simple verb/noun combination followed by a "from what …" "to what …" "by when … for example "Increase Product X sales from £1 million to £1.5 million by November 2017". In this way we have a strategic *speed* in a given *direction*. The *direction* being "Increase Product X sales" and the speed being "by November 2017". We also have a *measure:* "from £1 million to £1.5 million". If this format for whatever reason is deemed inappropriate, ensure that the Vital Few are at least expressed in a SMART way (Specific, Measurable, Achievable, Result focused, Timed).

It may help you if initially you capture the ideas on a flip chart (boy, do I love them).This will allow you and/or your team time to brainstorm possible suggestions as to what they believe their Vital Few issues should be for the forthcoming year. I would encourage you to adopt clear and simple phraseology. Keep it Simple. No long sentences!

Once you have done this, it is time to work out which of the draft Vital Few growth breakthroughs you or your company should adopt. Firstly, recognise the reality of the situation. If these truly are big breakthroughs, then you or your company can only realistically execute a handful of them.

Whilst it may be difficult at times for you and/or your team to curb their enthusiasm, any more than four "Vital Few" breakthroughs runs the risk of becoming impossible to execute even in a large organisation.

As mentioned before, work hard to select an appropriate number that will provide sufficient stretch and catapult you to success. Remember sometimes 'less is more' and this is one of those occasions.

To help you decide which Vital Few to proceed with, concerning the nature of the breakthrough, they must be high level, high-growth orientated and strategic in nature. They should be set with understanding and belief they can be achieved, not just bravado. Typical "Vital Few" examples which deliver step changes in growth could include issues like:

- Increase sales turnover with existing customers from £1 million to £1.5 million by November 2019

- Achieve £0.5 mil turnover from new export strategy by July 2019

- Generate £400k from the launch of new product X by year end

- Win a £600k contract from the aerospace sector before Dec 2019

- Reduce delivery times from 5 days to 3 days by June 2019

- Acquire a £3 million competitor in the professional services industry before year end

- Secure £1.5 million growth capital to expand production capability by March 2019

If we now call the agreed Vital Few the "Whats" (- *What we want to achieve*) we must now establish and agree the Hows *(- How we will achieve the Whats*).

Taking each selected "What" in turn, brainstorm what you believe the key drivers of execution are for this strategy, considering what important things you must make happen in order to convert this aspiration into a reality.

Try to tease out two, three, or four things that – if done well – would lead to the natural accomplishment of the "What". Again, try and ensure that you and/or your team are selecting the relatively small number of top level drivers not just generating long list of lower level tasks.

Let's use a simple analogy of losing weight to demonstrate the model.

Achieve these → & This will look after itself	**EAT LESS FOOD**	**DRINK LESS ALCOHOL**	**INCREASE EXERCISE**
Vital few	1	2	3
REDUCE WEIGHT FROM 13 STONE TO 11.5 STONE BY JUNE	*	*	*
Measure	Calorific intake per day	Number of alcoholic units drink per week	Time duration in minutes and frequency per week
Target	1500	5	20 & 3

WHAT (Vital Few): To reduce weight from 13st to 11.5 stone by June.

HOW: Eat less; drink less; exercise more

MEASURE: Reduce Calorific intake per day; reduce number of units of alcohol; increase number of workouts and time of workouts

TARGET: 1500 calories per day; 5 units of alcohol her week; exercise 20 minutes 3 times a week

If you're going to reduce weight from 13 stone to 11.5 stone and you want to do it by June you quite obviously have to eat less food, drink less alcohol and probably do more exercise. So those are the things you need to do.

The vital thing is what you're trying to achieve – your WHAT.

How you're going to do it is to eat less, drink less and increase your exercise – Your HOW.

Reduce calorific intake per day to 1500 – your Measure & Target 1

Reduce alcohol intake to 5 units a day – your Measure & Target 2

Increase Exercise duration to 20 minutes, 3 times a week – your Measure & Target 3

It is pretty straight forward so what I'd like you to do is to take three or four of those things from your Vision Maximiser and plot them.

Here is another more business-related example of a company plotting its one year plan:

Turning on Your Profits Tap | Steve Jones

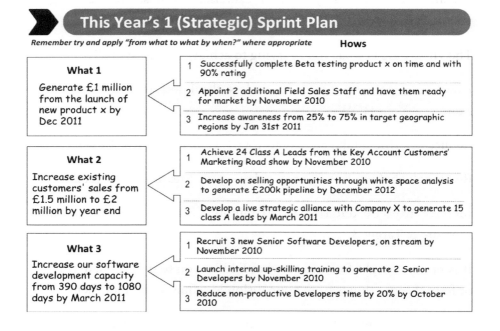

Now populate your One Year Sprint on the one page plan poster below.

Write in the "WHATs" in the left hand rows and the corresponding "HOWs" across the top columns and confirm the target measures in the lower columns. An example of this can be seen overleaf.

Now take these and transfer them to the diagram below.

Single Page Plan for:

			P1	P2	P3	P4	P5	P6	P7	P8	P9	P10
		SUPPORTING HOWS										
		By Whom										
VITAL FEW	VF1											
	VF2											
	VF3											
	VF4											

* Completely Relevant
O Contributes
Leave blank if doesn't contribute

	P1	P2	P3	P4	P5	P6	P7	P8	P9	P10
Measure										
Target (by when)										
Performance										

Notes on Performance
Green — Going to plan
Amber — Needs some attention
Red — Not going to plan. Project might not be completed in time

Write in the "WHATs" in the left hand rows and the corresponding "HOWs" across the top columns and confirm the target measures in the lower columns. Use an A0 blank template version if it helps.

Check alignment of WHATs and HOWs. In this new One Page Plan poster format, it becomes apparent that some of the HOWs will impact not only on the WHAT they were selected for, but also influence the other WHATs to a greater or lesser extent.

Going through each WHAT in turn, input a **star** to signify where it is a Primary (important) driver of the WHAT, a Secondary (indirect) driver. Or, leave it blank where the HOW in question bears no impact on the execution of other WHATS. This symbol is inputted where the HOW and the WHAT in question intersect. Each HOW will be a Primary driver for at least the WHAT it was originally selected for, so these symbols can be marked on straight away.

Once this grading has been completed for each HOW across the grid, you can bring to the attention of the team those HOW projects which have biggest impact across all the WHATs. In other words, via this process, you will discover the things you can do that will have the greatest impact on achieving your goals. It is a form of advanced priority-setting. that makes it possible to gauge which HOWs have the greatest impact on the execution of the One Page Plan. For example, if a particular HOW is a key driver of both the WHAT it was selected for plus another and possibly a secondary driver of a third WHAT, it can be seen to be particularly instrumental in the successful implementation of the overall plan. Due to its relative importance, this may influence who the team nominates to deliver this HOW project and the level of resources they are provided with.

Next, allocate Project Champions. For each HOW select a person responsible for the delivery of that project.

Finally, you'll need to monitor progress regularly, so completing the monthly Traffic Light performance indicator will help.

Due to the vital role this one page plan, what I call a *One Year Sprint*, will play in helping you or your company chart its successful high growth journey, I recommend that the plan is reviewed regularly each month. It will bring clarity and immediacy to your growth.

Project Champions should be challenged as to what degree their HOW project are on target. If it is just you, then I recommend finding a coach or someone to hold you accountable. Writers, who are largely considered to be solitary workers, creating stories and articles in isolation, often talk about how their spouse, editor, or even friends hold them accountable to producing more work, and how that is instrumental in helping them finish projects.

If everything on the HOW project is on target and proceeding to planned milestones, its box is shaded green. If the HOW is just off target and planned milestones, it is shaded amber. If considerably off target and planned milestones, shade red.

By adopting this highly visual review technique, it drives the agenda for review meeting.

If you have projects that are in red then they can get immediate attention they need and not get missed.

The Champion explains the action plan to get the project back on track and this can be supplemented by additional suggestions or offers of assistance from others in the team. Amber projects can also be subjected to a lower level of attention and those that have green projects are thanked for doing a great job.

Develop an Action Plan for each HOW project. In order to ensure each HOW project is delivered on time and to specification, those

Champions responsible for HOW projects will need a robust action plan in place to ensure they help make "it" happen. As these are deployed and aligned to the Vital Few issues, you can be fairly sure that failure to execute a HOW project puts the whole strategy in jeopardy.

HOW can also be broken down into another single page plan for specific tasks so you or the team can easily see if, or when, the plan is on/off target.

Turning on Your Profits Tap | Steve Jones

So, which are the most important "How" projects on this plan?

Key

X = denotes Primary driver

0 = denotes Secondary driver

HOWS — Initiatives to drive execution of the Vital Few

WHATS — This year's "Vital Few" Breakthroughs		How 1 Successfully complete Beta testing product x on time	How 2 Appoint new Field Sales staff	How3 Implement direct mail campaign to new geographic regions	How 4 Deliver the "Road-show" workshop programme for key customers	How 5 Develop on-selling opportunities with existing customers via "White Space" analysis	How 6 Develop Strategic Alliance with AB Limited	How 7 Recruit Senior Software Developers	How 8 Launch Internal Training Programme to up-skill Junior Developers
Champion		Bob	Sue	Bob	Lee	Bob	Bob	Sue	Sue
VF 1	Generate £1 million from the launch of new product x by Dec 2011	x	x	x	o	o		o	o
VF 2	Increase existing customers' sales from £1.5 million to £2 million by year end	o	x	x	x	x	x	o	o
VF 3	Increase our software development capacity from 390 days to 1080 days by March 2011						o	x	x
Target measures — from what? to what? by when?		A minimum satisfaction rating of 90% completed by March 2010	2 additional Sales people ready for market by November 2010	Increase awareness from 25% to 75% by Jan 31st 2011	Generate a minimum of 24 Class A leads by November 2010	Generate pipeline of £200k of new opportunities by Dec 2010	New Partnership to develop a minimum of 15 new "A Class" opportunities by March 2011	3 new Developers on-stream by November 2010	2 up-skilled to Senior Developer standard by October 2010

Traffic Light Review

- On or above target
- Marginally below target
- Significantly below target

Traffic Light Performance Indicator

You can take any WHAT or HOW project and break it down again and then again. What'll happen is that it should all repeat back to the master plan. So this way you can cascade your breakthrough plan through the business, through the departments, through the relevant teams or projects and feed back into the higher level.

To conclude, a high growth business with no strategy looks a bit like this.

A high growth business with no strategy

A high growth business with a strategy but not aligned or agreed looks like this.

A high growth business with a Strategy but not aligned or agreed speed

And with the work we're doing, we hoping that the ride is a lot more fun and that everybody is onboard and aligned.

2. RELEVANCE

It is so important these days to assume nothing, but rather to check in on whether the product/service you intend or are supplying still has relevance.

I see a lot of start up businesses emerge because the founder believes they have an offering that the world wants, without doing some due diligence first. The example I always quote is: How successful do you think you'll be selling typewriters in today's society? Unless you have a vintage market, I'm guessing you'll struggle.

Always check to see if your product/service is going to be in demand by undertaking some research and due diligence. This is why you see marketing left, right and centre as clients look to find out what it is consumers want.

This is as important to start up businesses as it is to the most established businesses.

You only have to look to the demise of institutions like Woolworths, British Home Stores and companies like IBM. If you take your eye off the relevance of your product or service to the market place you are tempting fate.

One thing is constant and that is change. Never more so that in today's business world. Take my industry for example:

At the time of writing this book we've had the uncertainty of Brexit which has slowed business.

We've also had situations where many coaches and trainers were running thriving businesses as the result of a government initiative called Growth Accelerator, designed to subsidise coaching and training to the SME marketplace. It was a hugely successful programme that was cut short by a government minister a year and a half early.

These coaching and training businesses were seriously impacted negatively when the government pulled the plug on the programme a year and a half early, essentially putting many coaches and trainers out of business and leaving their clients high and dry.

Currently, the challenge facing many training organisations in the UK, is the introduction of the Apprentice Levy. This states that companies with a £3m payroll cost must invest 5% of that payroll cost to the apprenticeship scheme. At first glance that might seem like a training company's dream. However, unless you are an approved government supplier you will not be able to service the need. At the time of writing no supplier list is available thus putting many training businesses out of business. It also forces these companies to spend this training budget in a prescribed way or lose it as a tax. Thus, other essential training will now get cut.

Finally, in my industry, how long before training information is accessible via the internet for free? I wonder.

If you look at other industries you'll see significant changes on the horizon.

In our lifetime we'll see driverless vehicles. What impact is that going to have on any person who earns their living driving? What impact will that have on the transport industry as a whole?

If you look at the utilities industry, what changes are coming as fossil fuel becomes a scarce commodity and climate change dictates a greener environment? The move away from fossil fuel to different forms of energy will have a profound effect and reshape the industry.

Technology is also going to change the way business is done. You only have to look at the impact of the internet on traditional retail. You have Amazon not only impacting the high street, but also setting the tone for all businesses in terms of expectation of delivery speeds. We now expect a similar service from all businesses. You have Kindle too, impacting book resellers and libraries.

In all of this it is really important to continually ask yourself:

How relevant is my offering?

Below is a neat tool that can help you think in a constructive way around this issue. It's called a PESTLE Analysis.

PESTLE analysis
is a useful tool for understanding and assess the situation of an individual business or organisation

PESTLE stands for "Political, Economic, Sociological, Technological, Legal and Environmental" factors.
The questions to ask yourself are:

What are the key political factors likely to affect the industry?

What are the important economic factors?

What cultural aspects are most important?

What technological innovations are likely to occur?

What current and impending legislation may affect the industry?

What are the environmental considerations?

Skills for
Business

One other exercise you might want to conduct as a business owner or as a team is the better known SWOT Analysis. This looks at internal strengths and weaknesses plus external threats and opportunities. Both are excellent exercises but when looking at relevance I prefer PESTLE.

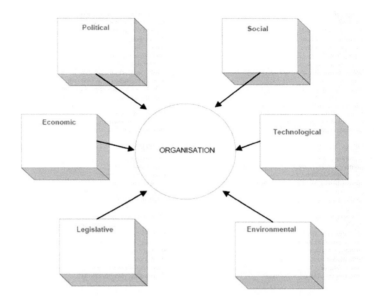

STRENGTHS
•Advantages of proposition?
•Capabilities?
•Competitive advantages?
•USP's (unique selling points)?
•Resources, Assets, People?
•Experience, knowledge, data?
•Financial reserves, likely returns?
•Marketing - reach, distribution, awareness?
•Innovative aspects?
•Location and geographical?
•Price, value, quality?
•Accreditations, qualifications, certifications?
•Processes, systems, IT, communications?
•Cultural, attitudinal, behavioural?
•Management cover, succession?

WEAKNESSES
•Disadvantages of proposition?
•Gaps in capabilities?
•Lack of competitive strength?
•Reputation, presence and reach?
•Financials?
•Own known vulnerabilities?
•Timescales, deadlines and pressures?
•Cashflow, start-up cash-drain?
•Continuity, supply chain robustness?
•Effects on core activities, distraction?
•Reliability of data, plan predictability?
•Morale, commitment, leadership?
•Accreditations, etc?
•Processes and systems, etc?
•Management cover, succession?

OPPORTUNITIES
•Market developments?
•Competitors' vulnerabilities?
•Industry or lifestyle trends?
•Technology development and innovation?
•Global influences?
•New markets, vertical, horizontal?
•Niche target markets?
•Geographical, export, import?
•New USP's?
•Tactics - surprise, major contracts, etc?
•Business and product development?
•Information and research?
•Partnerships, agencies, distribution?
•Volumes, production, economies?
•Seasonal, weather, fashion influences?

THREATS
•Political effects?
•Legislative effects?
•Environmental effects?
•IT developments?
•Competitor intentions - various?
•Market demand?
•New technologies, services, ideas?
•Vital contracts and partners?
•Sustaining internal capabilities?
•Obstacles faced?
•Insurmountable weaknesses?
•Loss of key staff?
•Sustainable financial backing?
•Economy - home, abroad?
•Seasonality, weather effects?

Skills for
Business

3. OUTCLASS THE CROWD: POSITIONING

This brings us to the next section which is all about 'outclassing the crowd' with your product and positioning. So having established your vision, we're now going to look at your product and positioning. This is how you 'outclass the crowd' and this is how you take advantage in your market place.

Let's start with some questions for you.

- How do you currently generate your leads?
- What are the quality of your leads?
- How many do you typically convert?
- How do you get past the gatekeeper?
- How many referrals do you get?
- Do you have raving fans who refer you everywhere?
- Are you know as the No 1 provider of your product or service?

Some interesting questions there that I hope made you think. Let's just look at that again.

How do you currently generate your leads? So, are you making cold calls? What are you doing to generate your leads and then when you get in front of the client, *what's the quality of the leads?* Are you having cups of tea with people who'll never buy your service? When you do get in front of those leads, and they are the right ones, *do you typically convert them?* How quickly are they buying your services?

How do you get past those gatekeepers? Gatekeepers are the people that prevent you from getting to the key person you need to sell to. For example, let's say you need to get to a Departmental Head or Business Owner to make the decision on your product. Quite often they've got very good protective lairs, like Personal Assistants or mid-level managers, so you can't contact them directly. If you can't get to them, how can you sell? It's important to consider how you get past those gatekeepers.

How many referrals do you get? When you're working with clients, are you getting referrals, did someone feel they just *had* to recommend your service/product to someone else? *Do you have raving fans who refer you everywhere?* Do you see people commenting on your Facebook or Twitter page? How are your customer reviews looking? Do your telephone staff report positive feedback? *Are you known as the No 1 provider of your product or service?* Are you getting ranked above your competitors in magazine columns, online polls and the like?

These are some of the questions we're going to start answering to get your 'positioning' clear. In subsequent chapters on Finding Clients 'lead generation' and 'Inspired Sales' we'll cover these questions again from specific angles.

I can't stress how important this section is. If you can 'Outclass the Crowd' and Position yourself for success, then your only challenges will be on how you manage the influx of new businesses that want your service.

Here are some key questions to consider as we find your market positioning

- Are you running a boutique service: small, profitable or is it a scalable thing? What business are you in? Scalable means everywhere. Fitness First was a scalable business. Boutique might be one fitness club as a contrasting example.

- Are you a lifestyle business or 24/7? I have a client on the south coast who windsurfs all summer and works all winter. Lucky guy as he is a lifestyle business that generates enough revenue during his 'on' period to live through the downtime. What business are you in? Is it lifestyle or is it 24/7? Are you working really hard?

- Do you intend to keep your business or do you intend to sell it? I have clients who have a five year strategy to build their business and sell it. Build their businesses, tread on the big boys toes and get bought out. A deliberate strategy. What are you intentions? To keep it, pass it onto the next generation or to sell? What are you intending to do with it?

- Is it about income now or is it about building value for later? For some people it's all about making money now, for others it's about building equity, a business of value. Neither are wrong. Some businesses like financial services are building residual income over time. For them the more clients they take on, the more people they have paying them a monthly fee. If they build this over time they will have a bank of people paying them money, a book, so that's an equity model. An income model would be "I'll sell you this and then I'm going to move on". None of these are right or wrong but what is your business about? Is it price driven or is it value driven? We'll talk a little more about this later.

- Is your business a Lidl or a Waitrose? Do you pile it high, sell it cheap or is it very expensive and available to a very few?

So those are some questions to ask yourself as we begin to design your positioning strategy.

Skills for Business

What business you are in will determine Strategy you adopt

- Boutique v Scaleable?
- Lifestyle v 24/7?
- Keep v Sell?
- Income now v Equity later?
- Price/Value?

© Copyright 2007 Steve Jones

Now what is positioning and what does it mean?

Do you remember earlier, in my introduction where I talked about remembering the school bully? The person who was a great sportsman/woman? The class egg head? They created that position in your mind.

It is no different in business. People/customers will be creating a position/picture in their minds about you and your service. The trick is to make sure they create the right position/picture around what you do. It is thinking in reverse. How do you want them to think about you and your service? And how do you now go and create that position/picture?

Do you remember my other example? Let's look at it again, for the sake of reinforcing what we know: If you saw a silver tray in a car boot sale what would you expect to pay for it? 50p -£5. Now if you saw that same silver tray in your high street jewelers what price then? £30 - £50 maybe. Now what if you saw that exact same silver tray, pride of place in Harrods Store in London – what price would you expect to pay then? £100 - £1000 maybe.

The point here is it is not the product but the positioning of the product in your mind. The same goes for you and your business.

To explore this further I'm going to use some famous people and ask you to think about the positioning these people created for themselves and hold in your mind?

So you've got:

- Stelios - Easyjet. What position has he created? He's a modern day Freddy Laker who wants to look after the people and make it affordable.

- Maggie Thatcher – the Iron Lady. My way or the highway so quite clearly you can see her strategy and you wouldn't mess with her - and she created that position around herself.

- Anita Roddick, Body Shop. Sadly, she's no longer with us but if you remember what she stood for, she was all about 'ethical' products. She wouldn't have anything tested on animals. That was her belief, that's was what she stood for and that's what she was known for.

- The Pope is an interesting one. He's the only one of these individuals who position has already been established for him, making him different to everybody else on this platform. He has a self made positioning. Most establishment bodies are good at this (in fact, they rely on it). The policeforce is another example of this preconception in action. Even the average, anonymous police-officer has authority because of what they represent and the institution they serve. Interestingly, however, these preconceptions are getting challenged more and more these days. Think of how many people actually *trust* the police now versus 50 years ago.

- Richard Branson, the People's Champion. Everybody loves him; he's got his island and all his staff go there. So you kind of get a feeling of what Richard Branson stands for.

- Alan Sugar. Equally as successful as Richard Branson but a completely different style. My way or the highway, always that pointy finger. He's interestingly repositioned himself of late, as the face of Apprenticeships. It's interesting as we have one generation who know him as the face of Apprenticeship and another that remember his Amstrad days where he was robust and you didn't get in his way.

- Nelson Mandela. He went to prison for his principles.

- Hitler – a very controversial character but one of the greatest motivators that ever lived, but with the wrong intent. When you look at what he was able to do, he made himself known for sure.

- Bill Gates. His vision was to have a lap top on everybody's desk. Now he's in third world countries giving his money away. Again, a very clear position, you knew what he stood for.

These are all people, like you and I, who have deliberately created a market position for themselves.

When we consider the Pope (or the police for that matter), it is interesting because due to the way in which they create their positioning, they have the best succession plan in the world. It doesn't matter who wears the uniform, the business continues. That's what you're aiming for too: a businesses succession that is uninterrupted and undiluted. It's the same with the Monarchy of any country – "The King is Dead. Long Live the King"

Everyone else in this example is self-made. They created a persona around them, a position that people understand. For one reason or another, people buy into this (or not) for personal reasons.

This is important because the stronger you can make the link between your business/ you and your product, in the eyes of the world, the easier it is for people to remember you and buy your products/services. You want your name or business to spring to mind when they think about your product/service.

So thinking about yourself, what do people say about you? A little bit scary, isn't it? I've been there and it's quite funny when you ask your clients. Quite often they will surprise you (not in the least because of how honest they can be!). What you think and what they think can be vastly different. But remember, perception *is* reality.

So if you think about positioning now, it's thinking in reverse. It's the position you hold in the mind of your clients. More importantly, establishing the correct position in the mind of your client. Your clients will have their views on you and your business and you may well be oblivious to them.

What you want is almost a congruent view; you want everybody thinking the same way. Therefore, you have to think about is establishing the correct position in the mind of your client.

All those people you saw in the example previously worked very hard to create their position, so that people/clients clearly understood what they did and stood for. That's what I want you to do with your business. I want you to create that image so that people get you and get what you do.

It's all about focus. Let's get clear on what your positioning is:

- How do you get in your clients mind?
- How can you make an impact in a saturated market place?
- What is your defense mechanism against a saturated market?
- What is the answer?

It doesn't matter what you do, there're thousands of people also doing it, unless you're very lucky. I'm a business coach. When I go networking, there are usually ten business coaches in the room and one business, and I've got to separate myself and stand out from the crowd.

So what is the answer?

There are plenty of things you can do to get noticed, such as going on the radio, running email campaigns, advertising, but if you're not strong in what you're saying around your business, not strong in what you believe, not strong in standing out from the crowd, it'll only lead you to having cups of tea with people who don't want your service. So how do you get into the client's mind with the correct message? It's so critical to everything you do when generating revenue and becoming profitable.

The answer is to focus on the perception of the client not the reality of the product. It's thinking in reverse. It's not your product; they can buy your product anywhere. They are buying *you*, how you make them feel; what you do; why *you're* different - not your product. That's a bit of a difficult one to get your mind around but actually it's true. Take my business. People can buy coaching from anybody. Therefore, it has to be the perception around me they're buying not the product.

So let's take this a step further. Let's look at markets we know of where there is definitely heavy competition.

Let's look at how supermarkets tackle this issue. Think of all the supermarkets you know and write them down. There are loads of them and they all sell the same thing essentially.

Here is a list I made:

Lidl
Aldi
Morrison
Waitrose
ASDA
Sainsbury's
Cooperative
Marks & Spencer

I could go on. There will be plenty more. Now, what people do is they create ladders in their minds around these supermarkets. You even get customers coming out of Aldi and putting their shopping in a Waitrose shopping bag to walk down the street. What's that all about? – *Perception* or should I say *Positioning*.

Some people will never walk into Lidl and will only ever shop at Waitrose. Some people will never shop at Waitrose and always walk into Lidl. These supermarkets know this and they design their strategies to attract the people they want, their market sector, their market share. Without realizing it, we create these ladders in our minds.

Lidl and Aldi are very good products but very affordable and Waitrose are very expensive. Morrisons are moderate and Asda and Sainsbury's are affordable, so they are all creating a price points here in our minds.

ans like:

"live a little, live a lot",
"every little helps"
"don't change your lifestyle, change your supermarket"

Look at the difference in their marketing campaigns. Morrisons will advocate fresh fish, their expert fishmonger and local produce. Waitrose will not mention the price, just inundate with sensual images of dripping chocolate or the like.

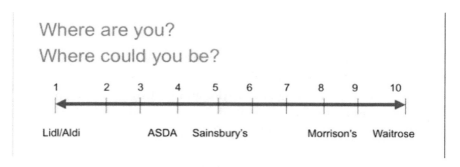

They all sell the same thing. What they are doing is actually sending their message to you around where to buy the same product so at the bottom end it's pile it high/sell it cheap and at the top end it's very expensive, and it's all designed, packaged, and sold to you in a way that is attractive.

So let's look at your product now. Where are you and where could you be on this spectrum? Who are your competitors, where are they? You might do a repositioning here. As I mentioned, as a business coach, there's a lot of competition. To give examples, a couple of organisations to mention are Action Coaches and Shirlaws Business Coaching. I've had to think very carefully about how I position what I do in order to attract the right client.

I'm more of a seven or eight, I'd like to think. It's quality not quantity and I'm dealing with people who value what I do and are prepared to pay for it. Now in order to make my product available at a more affordable rate, I run 'online' courses or 'one to many' to hold that position but make it affordable resulting in being able to get the value to more people.

So, where is your positioning on this spectrum?

Let's take this a stage further:

What are the three tallest mountains in the world? You may be wondering why I'm showing you this but there is a purpose which will become clear.

The Tallest and the First

So you're probably thinking already Everest, K2 but you're probably wondering what the third one is. Is it Kilimanjaro or is it one of the others? Yes it's Everest; yes it's K2; and the third one is a mountain that grows out of the sea somewhere in Japan I believe.

Now name the three astronauts that landed on the moon.

Turning on Your Profits Tap | Steve Jones

The Tallest and the First

Can you name the three astronauts?

There's Neil Armstrong, Buzz Aldrin and the third one tends to escape people but was a guy called Collins - although I believe he stayed in the space capsule.

Most people struggle to name the third mountain or astronaut. Why this is doesn't really matter. What matters is that beyond the first two, people struggle to recall.

The reason I'm showing you this is that when people come to buy your services, if you're not in the top two/three, people aren't going to know you, aren't going to remember you and aren't going to buy you, so you need to be on their 'mind shelf' when they're thinking about buying your product or service.

This 'top two' system may seem a bit unfair, but when you look at the science and history behind it, it makes perfect sense and gives us a clue on what to do about it.

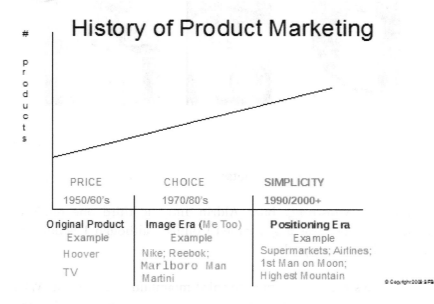

Original Product Era – me too era

In the 1950s and 60s it was very easy.
Hoover went down the street and they hoovered up. They sold a Hoover to pretty much everybody. The same with the TV. You didn't have to have brands; there were very few around and it was an era of original products.

Era of Image – 70's- 80's

At this stage, the marketplace became a little more saturated. Now it became about choice and the era of image. You had Nike, Reebok, Malboro Man and Martini. It became an era of celebrity endorsements. Celebrities were linked to products and 'feel good' factors were associated with products. People used their image to sell their products. You had the likes of Michael Jordan wearing Nike.

If you are old enough to remember Martini adverts on television, it was all about happy smiley people drinking martinis: "any time, any place, anywhere" was the slogan.

There was the Malboro Man on his horse on top of a mountain smoking his Marlboro cigarette. The message associated with this advert was simple, if you wanted to be a real man, the rugged outdoor type, you'd better smoke Marlboro Cigarettes. What was less known about this advert was that tragically four of the models subsequently died of smoking-related cancer.

The Era of Simplicity - 1990/2000+

Nowadays, it's all about simplicity. The market place now is so crowded. We are bombarded with messages every minute of the day via social media, email, television, and text messages. We even have adverts that follow us around after we've looked at them on a website – a strategy called re-marketing.

There are so many messages bombarding us these days, you have to have a very simple, very quick message that people can 'get'. Remember the supermarkets, airlines, highest mountain and man on the moon. You need to be on people's minds. Your clients have to be thinking of you when they want your service and they've got to know where to find you. So how do we get simplicity into our message so that we can get on our customer's 'mind shelf'? We need to look at Market Positioning!

Let's take airlines as an example.

Skills for Business

What's your market position?

Company	Product (What)	Market (Who)	Price (How Much)	Service (How Good)
	↑	↑	↑	↑
	↓	↓	↓	↓
What's your position?				

© Copyright 2009 SFB

Let's go back a few years, looking at British Airways and Easy Jet, and let's assess these two different airlines' market positioning with the following framework:

PRODUCT – What do they do?
MARKET – Who do they do it for?
PRICE – What do they charge?
SERVICE – What levels of service to they promise?

And use a simple scoring:
- HIGH
- NEUTRAL

- LOW

British Airways

PRODUCT: I think you'd agree it's high end. Quality Planes.

MARKET: The market it is aiming at is business class and high end market.

PRICE: You'd expect to pay for the quality product and service.

SERVICE: The service levels expected are high, with refreshments, attentive staff, and comfortable seating.

You can see they have an aligned strategy to create their positioning aimed at the high end traveller.

Easy Jet

PRODUCT: Second Hand Planes, Smaller Airports – therefore Low End

MARKET: Aimed at mass market and by default low end.

PRICING: They wanted to make it affordable so that anybody could fly with them; the price point was as 'cheap as chips'.

SERVICE: Their service levels were basic to non-existent – you bought your ticket online, you got a bucket seat from A to B and you were lucky if you got some food. That's changed slightly these days, but it is still not comparable to other airway service packages

So Easy Jet also have an aligned positioning strategy to attract a particular market, as do British Airways.

This is a generic example of two companies who do exactly the same thing but they do it in completely different ways. Because they do it completely different ways, they attract a different market.

Now if you are looking at this and your position. It boils down to those same four key questions:

What do you do?
Who do you do it to?
How much do you charge?
What service levels do you offer?

When you've answered those questions run the HIGH, NEUTRAL, LOW filter over your answers.

FITNESS FIRST PLC

I was with Fitness First Plc when they entered the fitness industry market in the UK and we had a mixed strategy at entry point. We knew that David Lloyd and Holmes Place were charging £70-80 per month membership at the time we started out. We also knew that it was too expensive for a lot of people but that there were still people who bought it. We also knew that the alternative model was a 'pay and play' leisure centre model at £3 a go, and you took your chances with the quality.

We therefore identified that if we could find a product that was affordable, but offered the same perceived quality as a Health Club like David Lloyd, we could corner the market. Fitness First launched their "affordable fitness" model in the late 90's.

PRODUCT: They had a high end product, with air conditioned spacious changing rooms, oak wood lockers, air conditioned, state of the art gyms, large airy aerobic studios with sprung floors to create a wow experience.

MARKET: Our market was mass market to attract high and low end users alike.

PRICE: It was all about affordability; our price point was so good that we could attract High End Users of more expensive clubs as well as Low End Users who previously could not afford a health club membership.

SERVICE: Our service levels were designed to recognize the client and give them a great experience. This required us to work hard to make their experience exceptional. We strove to create a club atmosphere that was unrivaled, vastly different to the competition, in order to corner the market.

The Positioning Strategy was to attract the aspiring health club members who previously could not afford a health club membership, whilst at the same time attract existing health club members of clubs like David Lloyd and/or Holmes Place by providing a much more affordable option.

This was how we managed to corner the market and become the fastest growing business in the UK, which led in turn to us becoming the largest health club chain in the UK, then Europe and eventually the World, all within a seven year period.

So what is your strategy? How are you going to separate yourself and outclass the crowd?

- Who are your competitors?
- Why are you different?
- What's their product, market, service and price and how can you position your business to get your market share?

Look at your competitors and see where your edge is. In order to find this out, if you're already in business, ask what makes you different? Why do people/clients buy from you and not someone else?

Values Triangle

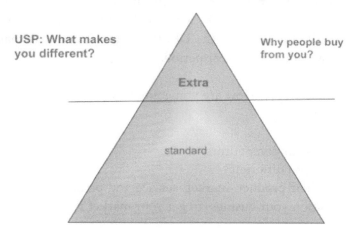

Let's take my current business.

There are thousands of business coaches out there in the market place, so why would someone buy from me? Why am I different? How do I stand out from the crowd.

I used to say the following:

I'm professional
I get results
I'm qualified
I'm personable
I'm affordable
I'm reliable

Now if I got all this across in a sales meeting you might think I'd get the business, which is also what I thought originally.

Here's the shocker though: A few years back, as I was leaving a sales meeting, the business owner whom I had been pitching to says, 'We are seeing six other coaches today so we'll let you know.'

'What are my chances now of getting the business?' I asked.

His answer: 'The truth is, at best slim.'

I realised at that moment that all the other coaches were going to say they are professional; that they get results; that they are qualified; that they are personable; affordable; and reliable. Of course they would. These were all standards, and I hadn't differentiated myself at all.

If in that meeting I could communicate that I have all of those qualities listed above *and* something else that makes me different, and that that something is the fact:

- I was part of the management team of one of the fastest ever growth business in the UK Fitness Fist PLC, and that we were opening a club a week at one point in the UK and 2 World Wide.

- That we went through the AIM and the Full Listing to become the largest independent health club chain all within a 7 year period

And then asked them if they thought I knew a bit about growing a business? What impression do you think that would make?

If I then explained that on leaving Fitness First PLC I worked with one of the fastest SME Specialist Coaching Business in the UK, Shirlaws International, and that all their methodologies, frameworks and coaching tools mirrored perfectly my Fitness First journey, giving me the experience and the toolkit. What chance have I now created to getting the business? Much better I would hope. Do you think my competitors can say this?

If I further compounded this by explaining that I have products that are unique around employee engagement, around motivation, and around business growth that actually aren't out there in the market place, I'm going to massively improve my chances.

If you are in any doubt as to your value then look back over your past achievements to see if you can identify your uniqueness.

I was once told:

'If you want to earn more money then tell a better story'

That's all I did and all you need to do. You see, I could have said that I used to work for Fitness First Plc, but what would that have meant? On the reception? Cleaning the gymnasiums? Instead, I've created my story, and shown where it all connects. They say the key to writing a good CV is telling a story with no gaps. If there are 'plot holes' in your CV, time that is unaccounted for, work that seems unrelated, it is going to weaken your story. Whereas, if your CV is watertight, and employers can see the clear journey from A to B, they can buy into the story.

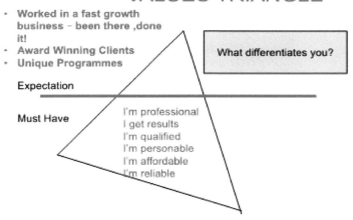

If you are still not sure, then ask your friends and clients to define your uniqueness. Ask yourself and them questions.

- Why do you think people buy from me?

Try also getting a colleague's view. Find your competitor's USP and differentiate yourself. There's no point in doing the same thing, that Unique Selling Point has already been taken.

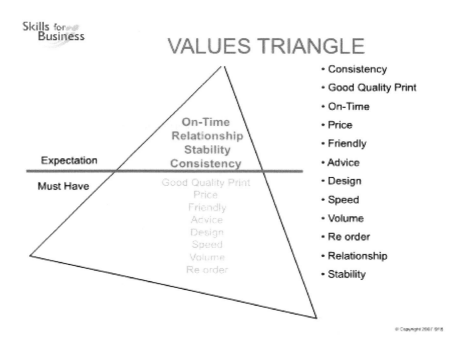

Here is a further example of a client that I worked with. They were a printing company. On the far right were all the things they said they did for clients. All I did was ask them why they are different. The differentiators appear above the line. Everything else is a standard and falls below the line.

VALUES TRIANGLE

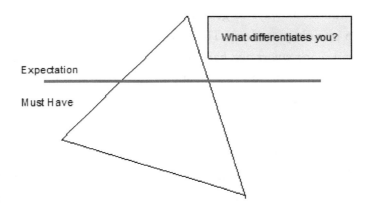

So now, when you are in front of an audience, or in a sales meeting, you can be very clear about why you are different. Once your clients know this, it makes buying you easier.

You should now be well on your way to creating a great positioning story.

You need to communicate it by finding the right clients for your message, as you are still the best kept secret until you do. Which leads (excuse the pun) nicely into the next chapter.

4. FIND YOUR CLIENT

There are numerous ways to generate leads. Far too many for me to mention in one chapter alone. Therefore, I'm going to take a look at how you can work *smart* not *hard* in your lead generation. I'm going to be talking about a more strategic approach which, if you do it well, will enable you to attract the right client at the right price.

This chapter is all about generating leads that call you. Lead generation for me is about 10 phone calls, 10 appointments, 10 sales. And they'll be calling you! That might sound a bit strange but it's really about how to build strategic alliances and key partners. Who are *your* supermarkets?

To explain this let's use Kellogg's Cornflakes as an example.

Do Kellogg's sell directly to you and I? The answer is 'No' they form a relationship with a supermarket who agree to display and sell their products.

You can apply the same principle in your business. Who are your supermarkets? My supermarkets are accountants, lawyers, IT companies and the like. They deal all day long with my ideal clients but don't do what I do. However, you can guarantee that these companies are in a position to recommend you, especially if their clients are looking for your type of service.

If you know how to build these relationships with these companies I call 'supermarkets' then when their clients are looking for my type of service, whose card do you think they'll hand them? Mine!

They'll probably go further than that, if I've built the relationship right. They will also tell the client to do what I say and pay what I ask. So in effect I'm pre-sold because someone else is referring me. This is what I call a 'Third Party' referrals and they are great.

It's not rocket science. If someone recommends a service and/or product they've used, you typically trust their judgment and proceed. It is the same in this scenario. It's no different to someone recommending a restaurant that they've eaten at.

In my business it works really well and there is no reason why it shouldn't work equally well for you.

When you build these relationships properly, you'll find that clients begin to ring you and ask you to come and see them. The good news is they already know what you do (because you've been positioned by your third party). They'll likely know what you charge too, but most importantly they will know you have the solution to their problem. This greatly improves your chance of winning the business. In actual fact I'd go as far as to say you'd have to *lose* the business. It also impacts your chances of getting your full fee, no questions asked.

This technique is so powerful that you can even make a few mistakes along the way as the trust is already built.

Another way of looking at this is that you get past the gate keeper (PA or Secretary), straight to the decision maker. Further to this, they know you've got the answer to their problem because you've been referred by someone they trust. When you get a few of these relationships going it really helps to accelerate the growth of your business. So, start to think: who are your supermarkets?

Relationship Building

Let's talk about how you find these supermarkets.

When I go networking I'm not really looking for an individual to work with, I'm looking to find these strategic supermarket relationships, these companies where I can build a trusted referral relationship.

You might well have tried this before and had little success with it. If that's the case there will be a reason for it which I'll explain in a while. Please don't give up.

I know the initial reaction to this approach from people who have tried it is that it has failed for a variety of reasons. They get excited, as we all do when a shining prospect is on the horizon, and it goes nowhere.

There are reasons why these attempts to build these relationships fail.

This is the usual scenario:

I go networking and I meet an accountant who has the type of clients

I'd love to work with. We agree to meet. I visit his office and spend time 'beating my chest' as I explain my business. Things are going well and the accountant agrees to refer me clients. At this point I'm pretty happy and anticipating great things!

However, what happens next is one of two things. I hear nothing (he probably puts my card in his desk draw with the intention of referring me, but forgets and discovers my card six months later). I call this 'neutral corner'. Or, worse still, the accountant refers me to his worst client, the least risk to him, his nightmare client. The type of client that moans and groans about everything. The type of client where you lose the will to live.

Relationship Building

Networking:

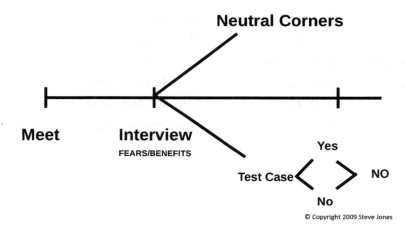

In both cases there is no relationship and no win either side.

Now the reason this fails is because actually there're some fundamental psychological fears which haven't been discussed. *The elephant in the room,* if you want.

So what is happening or not happening? If I sit in front of him and I tell him what I do, it's like 'beating my chest', the ritual of primordial apes, telling him how great I am. But in the back of his mind he's got fears around referring me. Unless I address those fears he's never going to refer me to his better clients.

In order to build these relationships properly I need to do something different in the initial meeting. I need to ask some different questions to flush out these fears. I don't beat about the bush. Instead, I'm very direct and ask "What are your fears of referring me?"

Now, I know there are 5 main fears and 5 main benefits to forming these powerful relationships and that unless they are discussed it is unlikely to succeed. I also know I've got to make sure I allay these fears and get rid of them before I'll get the relationship to where it needs to be for them to refer me their best client.

By asking directly what those fears are I can pick off his main ones and deal with them. He could say some or all of the fears below:

Skills for Business

Fears

- **Trust & Integrity**
  - Will you deliver what you say you will?
  - Will you respect their confidentiality?
- **Control**
  - Will they keep control of the situation?
- **Quality**
  - Are you as good as you say you are?
- **Consistency**
  - Can you deliver every time?
- **Time**
  - Is it worth the time they will invest?

Benefits

- **Financial**
  - Will you deliver a financial benefit –cost saving; profit; opportunity?
- **Loyalty**
  - Are you offering a relationship or just a transaction?
- **Network/Referral**
  - Can you introduce them to prospective clients
  - Do you have other products/partners/ suppliers they might use?
- **Knowledge**
  - Will dealing with you improve their knowledge in some way? – you're the expert!
- **Protection**
  - Are you offering them some kind of protection? Warranties; Support; Upgrades; programmes; future proofing etc.

© Copyright 2009 Steve Jones

FIVE FEARS!

1. Can they trust me?

2. How much control will they maintain?

3. Am I as good as I say I am?

4. Will I consistently deliver what I say I will?

5. Why should they give their time to this?

1) So the first fear is trust and integrity. Can they trust you with their

clients. It's taken them a long time to get some of these clients and they are giving them to you. So can they trust you? That's the first question.

2) Might be a fear about how much control they will have in the relationship.

- Will they keep control of the situation?

- Will you take their client and give it to somebody else who does what they do?

- How much control will they have? Will they know what's going on. Will you be telling them how you're working with their clients. Will you be involving them, because if fear is there they won't feel in control; then, they are never going to refer you a client.

3) The third one is the quality.

- Are you as good as you say you are?

They've only met you at a networking meeting and had a brief encounter with you. How good are you actually? Are you as good as you are making out? Do you provide a quality service and is it what their clients would expect? Are you going to let their clients down. I need to convince them that I am as good as I say I am; you need to show them that you are good, so it could be that you work with them first and then they refer you.

If they are a client first, then it would be like referring a restaurant you've eaten at, as opposed to one you haven't eaten at. I need at the very least to give them an experience of my products and services or allow them to speak with any/all my clients to get a sense of what I do so they are comfortable enough around my service to refer me.

4) The next one is consistency. Are you consistent?

Can you deliver every time? Would you be inconsistent and not show up? Would you lose interest? They can't afford for their client to not get a consistent service from you, especially if they have referred you.

5) Time. They are probably pretty busy so is it worth their *time* to invest in this relationship of referring clients?

These fears usually go un-discussed. You don't see the elephant. These are psychological fears that sit in the back of people's minds and are never aired, let alone addressed.

They are innate things and by getting them on the table and talking these through, I can put their minds at rest.

1) Trust: It may require me to work with them, give them access to all my clients, so they can ring them up.

2) Control: They may need to ask these clients if I've ever referred them to other people who do what they do. How much control do they want over the process? How would you like me to feedback

what I'm doing for your clients to you?

3) Quality: What's the quality of my delivery? Again, allow them to talk to your clients and see if they're happy with the quality of my delivery.

4) Consistency: Am I consistent? – do I turn up every time and do a good day's work with them. Again you can allow them to ask your clients.

5) Time: Is it worth their time developing this relationship? Helping them understand whether it's worth the time and effort for them to invest in me with their clients is often a big one. After all they are usually busy people. For the answers to this we probably need to look at the benefits to such a relationship of which there are 5 main benefits and these are linked to the fears.

The benefits are:

1) Financial: Will you deliver a financial benefit cost saving/profit/opportunity if you work with their clients. I'm a coach and if I improve their business, their profits will increase, their ability to pay their bills and to work with the client that's referred me will continue, so there's going to be a financial benefit on both sides. Plus, they would probably like to see their client improve and succeed.

2) Loyalty: If I go in and I do a fantastic job, that client is going to love the person who referred me to bits and ask if there's any other relationships or any other ways that they can work with them. So it's

going to enthuse loyalty as they look good in their clients eyes. Loyal clients don't stray far and are worth their weight in gold.

3) Referrals: The next thing is I can probably refer clients to them. I could introduce prospects and we can form a relationship where we can network and refer to each other. It's quite often the case that it starts in one direction but it comes back in the other direction so there're benefits for that person in receiving referrals too.

4) Knowledge: The other thing about these relationship is the knowledge exchange by working with their clients and by working with them. They will get a greater and a more in-depth understanding of how I do what I do and why people buy me. In fact, we'll both understand each other and our businesses better.

5) Protection: The final benefit will be protection. Their clients are going to go to a coach whether they like it or not, they are going to use someone's coaching service so isn't it better that they refer someone that they know and trust?

The alternative is their client finding a different coach that they don't know who then tries to take them and put them with a competitor of theirs. So there's protection built in as well.

Now when I'm building these relationships it looks like this:

Skills for Business

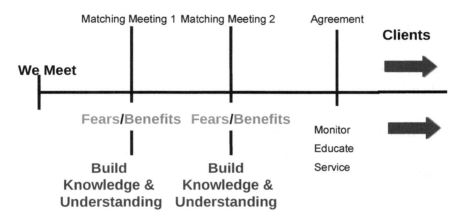

We meet, there are some fears and benefits to be discussed. We have a meeting around these fears and benefits. But I too need to make sure equally that my fears are discussed with them and the benefits of working with them are discussed also.

So we have two meetings – one on each side to discuss their fears/benefits they have around me and the fears/benefits I have around them.

It works like this: We meet, we have two rounds of fears and benefits, after which if we are still talking we move to an agreement. This can be a hand shake and an agreement to monitor, serve and educate each other over our referrals; it doesn't have to be a written agreement.

If this is managed correctly it should allay all fears and increase the chances of working with their best clients.

Now I've taught this to quite a few consultants and I know one or two consultants that run their entire business on this system. My business is mostly generated this way. It's a fantastic model and when it works you get put into the right client at the right price. They have the right issues that you can deal with. It's like having a free sales force. It takes a bit of time to work these relationships but the effort can feed you and your business for the rest of your life; it's really quite powerful.

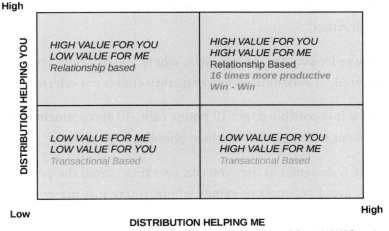

If you look at it from both sides, the distribution helps them and helps me:

High value for you and high value for me: It's a Win: Win – we both get value from it - – it's 16 times better and enables you to accelerate your business.

High value for you and low value for me (the referrer). On the odd occasion I've come across joint ventures where the referrer is not looking for new business but is keen to look after their existing clients. In this situation it's high value for me and low value for them. They're not really after anything so it works and interestingly is seen as high value to them as they see their client's benefit.

The ones that don't work are the bottom two, low value for you and low value for me which is transactional and as such, it's not going to work. Low value for you and high value for me is selfish so that doesn't work either.

So what you're looking for is a win-win, where you can refer and you can get referred. A relationship where quality clients are referred.

So that's how it is possible to get 10 phone calls, 10 appointments and 10 sales without making a call, by them phoning you.

This strategy is designed so that you can save time, avoid the perils of cold calling, avoid pointless meetings where you're just not going to get past the gate keeper, and situations where you're talking to people who just don't want your service.

Thus far we've done the vision, looked at product, looked at the positioning, we've had a look at lead generation, building the strategic alliances, so the next thing is sales and how to run a successful sales meeting.

5. INSPIRATIONAL & INTEGRITY-DRIVEN SALES

This is the sales part now; the power to influence. If you've been introduced to a client, in effect you are pre-sold - it's far easier! But let's look at sales in all aspects, whether you're pre-sold or not.

So what is the typical view of a sales person?

I expect you already have a clear image in your mind. If you are like me, you probably usually cross your fingers and steer clear, and as for sales calls, forget about it!

In fact any form of direct selling becomes an irritation. Now if that's your view of sales – and it's most peoples' view of sales – then it has a subconscious reaction when you're selling. Without you realizing it, it actually makes you feel uncomfortable in a sales role.

This is why most people don't like selling, because actually it's the subconscious connection people attach to selling. You may be one of the lucky ones who loves selling, however, I've trained enough individuals, business owners, coaches, consultant to know how true this is for the majority of people. This is why it's so important to have purpose and passion, because it's not like selling when you are passionate.

So, what if I told you I've never sold anything in my life but instead just built relationships? Yes, you'll think I'm mad. However, adopting this mindset really does change the dynamics. What if instead of selling you enter that meeting with the context of 'how can I help this person'? Then, your focus and energy are different.

Now, you are acting with integrity. There is real power is saying to yourself or your client – if I can't help you, I'll tell you, and leave the meeting.

With this approach, 'win or lose', your energy is not scattered.

You see, if you go in with the mindset to sell, then it is *your agenda* not *theirs*. If you win the sale you are buoyant. However, if you lose the sale, you are angry. This results in your energy being scattered as you are either elated or disgruntled.

When you put the client interest first, then win or lose, your energy is even, because you have simply identified a situation in which the help you have to offer is not appropriate at this time. Nothing is lost. It's called *integrity selling*. It's genuine, real, and authentic.

If you adopt the attitude that you're there to build a relationship with a client, then you are in a state of 'wanting to help them' rather than the more traditional mindset of having an 'intent ' to sell, or a "hidden agenda".

If you are there to listen to their needs and respond in a way that might help, it is a sincere approach that will be appreciated by your potential client. It also means if you genuinely can't help them or they are not ready for your solution, the door is still open to revisit them again later when they have the need for your services. I've had clients ring me years later and say "I'm ready".

If they are genuinely not ready for your solution, be brave enough to walk away. This way you are staying congruent to your mantra of helping the client if you can; it's not forced.

Let's take this another stage further. What is selling all about? Well, if you look at what Ron Willingham wrote in one of his books, *Integrity Sales*, he said that selling is 85% emotion and 15% logic, so it's about motivating others to take a particular action.

What does that mean? Well, boys and toys! A typical example, if a child opens a box and they've got 52 toys, do they need all of those? No. Do they want them? Yes. So we buy in an emotional state and then we back it up with logic later. So bear that in mind as we're going through the sales process.

It starts with truly understanding what you are selling. You're not selling the product/service, you're selling the good feeling attached to it. Or in other words, what it will get, give or do for them. You are matching their needs and their wants, how it may make them feel.

For example: A new Firewall might make someone feel that they've got peace of mind and security. If they've got what you offer it gives them that inner security and peace of mind.

A beautiful car that screams "success" might make them feel as though they have prestige; they feel better about themselves and feel more self worth. All of these examples are feelings based. It's not to do with the product, it's how the product makes them feel. So you need to make people feel a particular way before they will say *yes* and that's really what you're selling. It's what it's going to get them, give them, or do for them that's the key here, not the product/service itself.

In order to do all of this you need to be able to build rapport. Rapport is the number one thing you need to be good at and that only comes from integrity and a genuine desire to serve others.

So, why do you need to build rapport? The quicker you get people to know, like and trust you, the quicker they will buy into you. Once a person opens up to you, you can accurately match their needs and wants better. People buy people.

Now, if you're a sole trader or you work by yourself, then it is even more critical. People do buy people. They can buy your product or service anywhere but they are buying you. They are buying you at an emotional level so you really need to, as Stephen Covey wrote in his book the *The Seven Habits of Highly Successful People*, "seek first to understand and then be understood". If you can understand what their needs are then you can match them and then you can get them to buy from you. It's quite straight forward really, but putting it into practice can be hard.

It's thinking in reverse: thinking about their needs and then matching their needs. This is key in any sales process, giving people what they want, not necessarily what they need.

Another thing that is vital to understand before visiting any potential prospect is to get your mindset right.

Before you go anywhere near a sales meeting, have a purpose and a context. Why are you going to that sales meeting? What is the purpose of you being there? What's your context? What do you want to happen? Do you know your product well enough? Do you know the outcome you want? Can you put yourself in the clients shoes so you can understand how they will see you and your approach? What objections might they have?

One of the greatest Neuro Linguistic Programming techniques I learnt a few years ago is called *perceptual positions* and it has really helped me put myself in the client's shoes.

This is what I do:

I imagine floating out of my body and floating into theirs. I imagine looking at myself through their eyes. This is simple visualisation. Use your mind's eye to give you the answers you need: Imagine what they see, how they feel, how they think, what they are looking for. How are they going to know, like and trust you? What sort of objections, if you were them, would you come up with? I find this process really helps me tune into the client and their potential needs and wants, and it is the act of picturing it in your mind's eye that frees up your ability to empathise.

If this process is a bit rich for you, then just spend time imagining and second guessing what the client will want from the meeting. Though this is more 'intellectual' than feeling based, it can still work. Once you've done this you can structure your meeting to cover off any concerns by including them in your sales meeting.

Quite often, as a result of doing this process, I'm able to inoculate against objections early on by raising their concerns before they do.

I call it an inoculation because it's just like a flu jab - which is a weakened form of flu given early - so that when the real flu comes or objection in this case, you have already taken the sting out of it by raising it yourself. When they raise the objection it has already been addressed.

Let me give you an example. Many years ago I was doing a presentation to 12 partners of a law firm. I knew I had my champions in the room. However, I also knew that as partners there would be those who find it easier not to have to make a decision, and finally there would be those who would be the devil's advocates and say *no* to anything.

In order to apply the inoculation early I included it in my opening statement.

"Thank you for taking the time to see me today. Before I go any further, I know I have been invited by X to present to you. I also know that sometimes it is easier to do nothing and I fully appreciate that, and I also know that when I've left and you are discussing what I'm showing you today there is always one person who will be the devil's advocate and say 'no'. I appreciate this is human nature. Now let me present to you"

In this particular case it worked like a dream. When the partner who was championing me called back, he said that when the devil's advocate started dismissing the presentation, the remaining partners called him on it straight away, thus neutralizing him, and they proceeded to accept the proposal.

In addition to this you really need to know and understand building rapport and be prepared to be flexible in your communication style. Not everybody communicates the same way. Learning how to be flexible with your communication styles will really help.

Remember this is all happening *before* you even go near a meeting.

To help you, sit down and make a list of all the benefits of what you are selling or doing. Sit down and write a list of all the benefits - everything. List all the genuine benefits that the client will get from you. All the reasons why you are better than your competitors, and remember that they can buy your service from anybody, so why are you better? What's unique. What's outstanding. Remember the positioning we did earlier.

Remember, all the reasons you are better than your competitors – make a list so you've got it to hand. That will make you feel more confident when you actually go into a meeting and help you manage any difficult questions.

Another way to do this, and again another NLP tool, is to think of a time when you made a really successful sale.

If you've had times in the past when you've made a really successful sale, or where you've done something really well, try and access that feeling. Try to recall and understand what caused that to happen. Were you confident, in control, did you feel calm or certain; what was it? Try and remember because that's what is coming across and what people are buying. They are not buying your product, they are buying your confidence, maybe your power, maybe your calmness or your certainty. People are buying those things and then the product. It will pay big dividends to really think about the times when you've been successful in those environments and to recall how you were feeling, behaving and what was going on about you that was making it work. This is another form of visualisation, in which the projected image in your mind *becomes* the reality.

To do this I recommend closing your eyes, recall that time and imagine floating into that former you. See what you saw, here what you heard, feel what you felt. Make them bigger, brighter, add more colour, what are you hearing? How are you feeling?

By accessing those feelings you can anchor them by physically squeezing your thumb and finger together. You can then re access them before your meeting, by repeating this movement, and take them with you going forward.

Just a note on building rapport, a key skill for sales…

Building Rapport

Why have I started this section on sales by talking about building rapport you may well ask! Well the answer is simple really: Without rapport it's unlikely you will sell anything.

Now I could write an entire book on this subject alone but instead I've picked out what I consider are the salient and key areas.

What does Building Rapport mean?

My definition of Rapport is your ability to get people to know, like and trust you, by minimizing the differences between you. This can be done in a conscious and/or unconscious way.

Whether we are aware of it or not we do this naturally anyway.

If you've ever been at an airport waiting for a flight and people watched you'll know what I mean. How easy is it to spot a couple of newly weds or people at early stages of love. It's almost 'get a room' stuff as they are so engaged. Contrast that with a couple not in the early flushes of love and you get a sense of what I mean by rapport.

There is an exercise I do with groups which demonstrates the ability to build and break rapport.

I divide the room by pairing people up. I sent half the room out of the room and brief the other half.

The group that stay in the room are the group who are going to question the group outside the room when they re-enter.

They are tasked with finding their partner again, sitting down and asking them to describe a recent holiday. What happens when they describe the holiday is they get very animated, they get very excited and there's lots of rapport going on between the individuals and then about three-quarters of the way through this rapport building, I get the individuals that are questioning to disengage.

I get them to get totally disinterested in the person, the holiday, to see how long it is before the person they are talking to dries up and can't talk about the holiday anymore. The reason they can't continue is because actually they aren't getting any positive feedback or any rapport. It always amazing how quickly the conversation dries up as most people can't last more than a minute.

Exactly the same will be happening in a sales meeting. If you don't build rapport and stay engaged with the client, there will be no sale. This is why it is so important to make the meeting about them not you as you'll see in my sales process later.

So we're looking here really at what's going on and what's happening. Without rapport you can't run a sales meeting.

So a question for you.

How much of your communication do you think is made up of words, tonality and body language?

You may already know this but a lot of people surprisingly don't and it has a massive impact on you as a person and your communication with other people.

So you've probably got some percentages in your head, you've probably written them down so let's see where we go with this.

According to a study conducted by Albert Mahrabian in 1960

7% is what you say, the words

38% how you say it, tonality

and 55% is body language.

When we speak, it is not just words. It's our tonality, it's our body language as well that people connect with. That's why telephone sales people are trained and encouraged to walk about and use their bodies when engaging over the phone with clients. It is said that you can hear a smile down the phone and I think we've all come across people totally disengaged or distracted on a phone call, without seeing their body language

Often what I tell sales people is don't sit at your desk, don't sit at your computer, walk around, use your hands, use hands free because people will pick up your body language and they will pick up your tonality.

What this actually means is that 93% of your communication is non-verbal.

Your potential clients are going to picking up the signals - there's an expression "you leak the truth from every pore" so people will know if you're not congruent, if you are not 100% behind your product.

I hope now you are beginning to understand the importance that everything you say (words), your tonality and your body language must be totally and fully congruent when you go into a sales meeting. This means that you must totally believe in what you're selling, as 93% of your communication is non verbal.

So it isn't what you say, it's how you say it.

Use tonality and body language to back up all you say.

Use everything you've got to create a congruent message. I've worked a lot on this area, and you can really drill down into it if you choose to.

Body Language - Now if you break this down further, body language is posture; gestures; facial expressions; eye blinking; even breathing.

If you can match the person that you're talking to in those areas by mirroring them it will help you build rapport. Why? Because at an unconscious level, unbeknown to them, you will be minimizing your differences. At a subconscious level they will see you as like themselves.

There's a little exercise they did years ago which actually emphasizes this point. looking at facial expressions and eye blinking. You might try next time you want to get served at a bar.

In a busy bar they took a £20 note and they flicked at the rate the bar person was blinking at and subconsciously they got served quicker than other people. Whether that's true or not doesn't really matter it's actually matching the individual as best you can in everything that they're doing without being too obvious.

Tonality – it could be the pace they speak at, do they speak slowly. The tone they use, the tempo, how rough they are in their timbre, the volume, the pitch, the tone, when they pause. If you can match as best you can the way they're talking so if they're speaking slow, you speak slow. If they're quite rapid, you speak rapidly. It's trying to match them without it being too obvious.

Words – words do play a part. Try and match their language and their metaphors for life. An example of this might be a client whose metaphors for life might be based on football. His language may reflect this. He may say things like: it's a game of two halves; so again you could start to match language like that with similar language with statement like: 'let's kick off with this' or 'what is your goal' or 'do you know the score right now'. Look out for key words that people use.

Also look out for common experiences. A good example here is you walk in and there is a picture of his family with three children and you've got three children - there's a common experience that you can associate with straight away. Or they go to the same school or the same university.

The final piece on building rapport I want to cover is their communication style and preferences.

Are they a someone who needs lots of details and explanations if so you'll need to be tolerant of that fact and spend time in detail.

Or are they someone who wants to skip the detail and get straight to the point. Someone who is fast moving impatient and just wants to know headlines and summaries. If so, involving them in detail will disengage them.

Or are they someone who likes to mull things over and doesn't make decisions fast. Someone who takes their time. Someone who won't make a decision until it feels right. Again be tolerant, otherwise you will disengage them too.

You will need to be tolerant of all three types. You may also need not only to match them first to build rapport but then to lead them.

By leading them I mean you may have to chunk up to the bigger picture for the person stuck in detail. You may have to chunk down into detail for the person who just likes bullet points and headlines.

So I'm hoping that this is making sense by using the full range of your communication skills (word, tone, and body) you'll be able to build rapport fast in any meeting not just sales.

It's all about congruency. If you don't believe in what you are selling, you won't be able to convey it in your non verbal communication. Now as I said before, we leak the truth from every pore. 93% of our communication is non-verbal which is a bit scary. Knowing your product makes you more confident and that exudes itself in your selling so be very clear about yourself as a person and what you're selling. It's going to have a massive impact on the outcome.

If you do all these things you should now be ready for that all important sales meeting. So, we are now going to cover how you run those sales meetings. Your Inspirational & Integrity Sales Meeting strategy.

Running The Sales Meeting

Now we come to running the sales meeting. What do you do in a sales meeting? Do you have a process? A lot of people I come across don't have a sales process. They'll go to a meeting and just run the meeting intuitively. That may work for them or it may not.

If it works then it's best to analyse the process that sits behind it, so that it can be repeated or taught to other sales people in the organization. Otherwise, it's a bit like baking a cake without a recipe. You might get it perfect first time, but with no recipe how will you repeat it?

I see this a lot in businesses. Usually there is one person, often the owner, that brings all the business in. They intuitively sell but have no idea how they do it. This isn't a problem initially, however, as the company grows the process needs to be defined and taught to others. Otherwise, later on, it becomes a limiting factor.

I have a process that I run that ensures that I cover everything that I need to cover in a sales meeting and no stone is left unturned. That's what I'm going to share with you right now.

It's a six step sales process and it's designed to be about the customer's agenda.

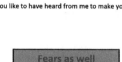

Sales Meetings
Six Steps to Success

1. **Agenda** – Remember, it's the **customer's** agenda
    - Global Agenda – Why the meeting was called
        - "What do you want to do today?"
    - Specific Agenda – Specific topics for today
        - "What do you want to achieve at this meeting?"
        - "By the end of this meeting what information would you like to have heard from me to make you feel we have had a successful meeting?"
2. **Positioning**
    - Pre-sold – Recommended or existing customer
        - Brief introduction to Skills for Business
        - Not Pre-sold – New prospect from marketing
        - More detailed introduction to Skills for Business
3. **Fact Find** - Just Listen – it's your turn next
    - Find out their requirements, problems and feelings
    - Include Business Needs Analysis
4. **Presentation** – Present to the **customers** issues
    - **Pause** – Don't break the silence!
5. **Summary** – summarise and confirm your offer
6. **Close** – Agree next steps
    - What you will do next
    - What the client will do next

SCI between each step
Summarise
Confirm
Introduce

Fears as well Benefits

© Copyright 2009 Steve Jones

1. Agenda

Right at the top agenda - Remember it's the customer's agenda so it's about them, not you.

Global Agenda - It's about building the relationship. It's good to be clear and know why the meeting was called. Did they call it or did you call it? It's wise just to remember that. Beyond that it doesn't really matter.

Specific Agenda – Straight away you can put yourself in the driving seat. In any situation, the person asking the questions is the person in control. Here you have a real opportunity to find out what they would like to get from your meeting by asking two simple questions.

"What do you want to achieve at this meeting today?"

"By the end of this meeting what would you like to have heard from me to make you feel that you've had a successful meeting?"

By asking these two questions you are going to get the clients entire agenda. As questions go these are two of the most powerful questions you'll ever ask, because in answering, they are going to give me everything you need to know and answer in that meeting.

Typically for me, the client will want to know things like:

What do you charge?

How long it will take?

Why are you different?

What are your payment terms?

Who else have you helped?

Are you qualified?

Will I be working with you or someone else?

It can be a myriad of questions. This step is so critical for two reasons. Firstly, you are listening to the clients needs and wants straight away – so they feel valued and listened to. Secondly, they are giving you their whole agenda and that's useful information. Now you have something to work with.

What typically happens at this stage is that there is a burning desire to answer those questions. Avoid this like the plague. Keep your powder dry. You are in a strong position as you now know exactly what they want from the meeting. In effect you've done a mini fact find on their needs and wants.

Avoid the knee jerk reaction to launch into answering those questions - avoid that with a vengeance.

You've now got their agenda so the next thing to say is:

"Thank you very much for telling me what you want to get from today's meeting." Then repeat what they have said and confirm it back to them. In other words:

"My understanding from what you say is that you'd like to know… is that correct? Thank you!"

At each stage of my sales meeting I do what I call SCI.

I *summarise* what's been said.

I *confirm* it with them and *introduce* the next section.

The purpose for SCI is to ensure and demonstrate that I have listened and that I am on the same hymn sheet before I proceed.

145

The link to the next step is this:

Before I answer your questions can I just confirm what you know about me?

2. Positioning

Now it's time to find out if you are pre-sold or they've just come across your business by chance. To determine this again it's about asking.

"Before I go any further, what do you know about my organization?"

This is the positioning piece - I need to understand: am I pre-sold? Have I been recommended by that accountant, that lawyer or IT company?

If I have, what did they said about me? I need to know how pre-sold I am so I can fill in the gaps.

If I'm pre-sold, what did they say about what I do? Did they really pre-sell me? Now all you've got to do is fill the gaps.

If you have been truly pre-sold it is a case now of you losing the business not winning it, because you've been highly recommended and you are the person who can resolve their issue, because a trusted partner said so. So you can see this positioning is pretty important.

But what happens if you are not pre-sold?

If you're not recommended in, then you're not pre-sold, so you'll need to have a positioning statement.

"Let me tell you a little bit about myself..." Then I tell my *positioning* story.

Now you have their agenda, and you've positioned your organization.

3. Fact Find

Now I'm going to conduct a further fact find, so it's their turn to start talking. I'm going to dig deep into the problem that they have identified they have that they think I can solve.

I'm going to start asking them lots of questions and sit back and listen.

I'm going to get into the fears and benefits of why this keeps them awake at night. If you can turn this around, what would it mean for your business? If we can solve this issue, what would happen, how would it help you?

Remember, I've got their specific agenda, they know what I do as I've positioned myself and I know what's going on with their business and what they're trying to achieve.

I'm now in a very, very strong position to present back to the customer based on this information and explain how I can help them, whilst at the same time answering all those specific agenda questions

4. Presentation

The presentation now becomes very simple.

Based around what they have told me they want from the meeting and the deep dive into the problem they face I'm now able to present back my solution and how much it will cost.

I'm even able to go back to the specific agenda on what would constitute a good meeting and tick off the answers to the questions they posed in front of them. This demonstrates listening skills: as you tick off their questions in front of them, it rarely fails to impress.

5. Pause and Summary

Summarising may sound something like this: "You've asked me these questions – how much do I charge, what do I do – have I answered all your questions? Is there anything I've missed?

"I've also shown you how I can help you. Is there anything else you need to know?" I then pause to allow them to digest what's been said and sum it up in their minds.

Sometimes in the summary, you may need to go back and re-emphasise or clarify some points, and then you move to the close

6. Close

It's now time to agree the next steps. Quite often I see sales people come away from sales meetings and they haven't agreed the next step.

This ends up leaving them in limbo when they don't hear from the client.

Make sure you are very clear on the next steps. This is how I do it:

"I've presented to you, and I'd like to know what you would like to do next?" Remember it's their agenda. They may need to think about it - check if there's anything you've missed or need to go over again. If not, it may be they genuinely just want time to think about it.

If that is the case allow them that time by asking "When will you have thought about it by?" Agree a time-frame, they may say by next week.

"Ok when next week will you have made your decision? Will you call me or would you like me to call you?"

If they agree to phone you by a certain day, please ask this next question.

"So if you haven't phoned me by next Thursday will it be ok if I phone you next Friday just to get closure?"

Here you are gaining permission to contact them and demonstrating that if it is not right they can tell you and you can both move on.

This way you are not left hanging around wandering whether you should call them. It protects your integrity.

On the other hand if they agree to proceed you need to outline clearly the next steps. I might help them by agreeing the next steps based around what they'd like to do. So it's all about them, not about me.

A word of warning about this Sales Process. You may have to be flexible with this process. It could be you'll walk into a business and they'll want to show you around. In this case, you are straight into the fact find.

That's fine, you can gather some information before you go back to the agenda, positioning, and then back to the fact find again later. Do your best and follow this process even if you have to move it around a bit.

If you do, it's a relationship based process which should give you great results, especially if you're pre-sold in the first place.

There are a couple of overlays on this model that it would be advisable to follow.

Summarise Confirm and Introduce

In between each of the steps, be mindful to *summarise* what has been said, *confirm* understanding from them, and *introduce* the next section/step.

Let's just jump back to the transition between the agenda and the positioning.

Summarise: "So my understanding is that you want to know x, y and z."

Confirm: "Is there anything else that you need to know from me today to have had a successful meeting?"

This ensures we are still on the same hymn sheet regarding:

- what has been said

- what has been understood

Then you can move to *introducing* positioning. Again, at the end: summarise, confirm and introduce. It maintains clarity throughout the process.

The summary, confirmation and introduction makes sure there are no misunderstandings as you go through this process. It also means you are documenting the conversation as you go through. If you follow this process I can pretty much guarantee that the clients will buy into you and your service if it's what they want.

5 Decision Points in Buying

There are 5 decision points in buying. I'm going to go through these because they are interesting and valuable to consider as well. You can remember the decision points in buying by using the acronym: DREAM.

Do they want it in the first place?

Repeat purchase – will they go back to their original supplier? If they have somebody they are already using you need to break that reason, so you need to differentiate yourself somehow – that is why understanding your positioning and being recommended are so critical.

Evaluate – looking around for a better offer. They may be talking to you but they may be looking for a better offer. Again if your positioning is strong and/or you are recommended it will put you in the driving seat.

Accessibility – can you make it easy and seamless for them to move across to you?

You only have to look at the Utilities industry. All utilities sellers now make it so easy to buy, and mobile phone companies make it so easy too. Banks are now doing the same.

If you have great processes in place you can become the accessible, seamless option. If it's clunky to move over to you, they may stay with their existing supplier. This is something to consider when you are in a competitive market.

Money – they will buy if they perceive the value outweighs the cost. You've got to demonstrate your value, why you are different, because that's what they will buy. Remember your value when going into meetings, why you're different and why people should buy you – your positioning again.

So it brings us to the end of this section.

P = We've done the purpose/vision,

R = we've looked at the importance of having a relevant product,

O = we know we've got to 'outclass the crowd' through our positioning

F = we know how find clients through strategic alliances to lead generation

I = and now you have an idea of how to run an Inspirational & Integrity Sales Meeting

T = the next phase we're going to talk about is how you manage your time successfully so you can deliver your service in a way that delights. So the next section is about your time management, your systems and processes, and we'll be looking at how your factory and your capacity operate.

6. TIME MANAGEMENT & CAPACITY

This section is about managing your personal capacity, your business capacity, and time efficiency, to drive your business growth. Now if you've done your positioning correctly, if you've done your lead generation correctly, you'll be in the right sales meeting and if you've run your sales conversions correctly then your challenge will be managing your clients and managing your time around your clients. This section is all about how to manage your time and your business effectively.

Now in this section I'm going to cover:

- how a standardized approach can scale your business

- building a standardized approach around processes critical to your growth

- identifying key business processes

- mapping and improving processes

I want you to think like we did in the introduction to the P.R.O.F.I.T.S. model. I want you to:

- Identify *7 things* on your "to do" list - things you do on a day-to-day basis that constantly appear on your to do list.

- Now pick *3 things* on your you 'wish list' – things that if you had time in your business you'd do, but you simply don't have time.

Once you've done this you should have a list of 10 things.

Your list might feature items such as emails, phone calls, meetings, conversations, clients. The 3 things on your 'wish list' might be things like: to get some time away from the business, maybe some "me" time, or even some projects you want to get on with. Maybe if you could you would go networking but you don't get the time. These are the sorts of things that should be appearing on your wish list.

When you started your business you probably didn't sign up for all of the things on your "to do" list, and they are usually somewhat removed from what you love doing, your passion. Nevertheless, they all need to be done by you or someone.

My intention is to simplify and make sense of these lists for you in a simple model.

I call the model the 'SOS' model and it stands for Support, Operations and Strategy. It's also called SOS because if you don't do these things, they'll come back to bite you later!

The model again is a contextual model that will help you make sense of the list you've drawn up really quickly, by attachment to the 3 clear areas.

First of all, you have a factory. My factory's output is "preparing workshops". Next, you have a *delivery mechanism* which ends up with the client, which you get paid for. I call this part 'Operations' and everything operational on your list will come under this heading.

It could be that you make widgets then deliver them to the end client. Everybody has a client of some sort which requires preparation (factory) and a delivery mechanism allowing it to end up with a client (operations).

SOS MODEL

FACTORY

⇩

DELIVERY (OPERATIONS)

⇩

CLIENT

In order for that to happen you need back office *support.* Back office support will consist of things like: admin; health and safety; compliance; HR; premise management; accounts; VAT etc. It is the support you need to run your business.

Now, the first thing I'd say about business support is that it tends to get in the way of delivery. If you able to outsource these functions I would recommend doing so as much as possible. If you do so it really does free up your time for other more important functions, the functions that enable you to earn your real money. This is important because it's not the best use of your time – no disrespect to people who are experts at this – it's not going to be as profitable as delivery and/or strategically growing your business.

You can easily outsource your HR, your admin, to a virtual assistant or HR Specialist who, in fairness, will be expert at it? You can even outsource your premise management. If you have an office why nor make it a serviced office where they take care of the premises for you? What else could you outsource? What could you get rid of? What could you get other people, who are more skilled, to do? This is all with the aim to make you free to do what you're good at which is the factory, delivery, and strategy.

I see far too many business owners doing their VAT at weekends, or grappling with an HR issue they are not qualified to deal with – all stealing valuable time from the business owner.

I urge you to make yourself redundant from these support tasks as soon as possible in order to be free to do the important stuff that grows your business and brings P.R.O.F.I.T.S.

Now there is a third dimension to this model that most business owners are prone to ignore, through lack of time.

In my experience many business owners look at their businesses as being Operations and Support only and neglect the critical third element.

Let's use my business as an example. I design workshops and deliver

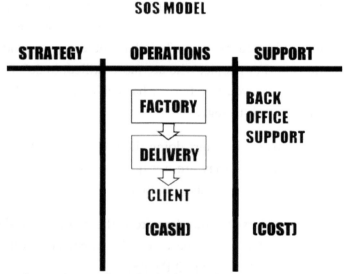

them – Operations – for which I'm paid. I perform all my back office support that enables me to do the operations. I run my accounts, do my VAT, manage my IT, issue invoices, answer emails etc – all of which is the support needed to run my business.

If I do this well, then I generate revenue through the operational aspects which result in clients paying me. However, if this generates the revenue, the support activities are viewed as the costs in running my business.

What does revenue – cost equal? Most people answer *profit*. However, it is not profit at all it is 'Product Margin'. It is the difference between what you get paid versus the cost of production. Now as businesses grow, if they are not careful, their costs increase and the product margin gets squeezed, which results in less and less profit. You will hear companies say things like: 'Turnover has trebled but profits have halved'

Why is this? Because their processes become more inefficient. You get double handling, duplication, things not getting done etc. So it is vital that you hone your processes and document them to maintain efficiencies.

However, even if you do this and do it well your business may not grow if you don't focus on the third element: *Strategy*.

This focuses on things that I've covered in this book, like positioning your business for success, distribution channels, getting pre-sold business coming in, joint ventures, partnerships, and also leveraging your pricing and product mix so there's lots of things you can do in strategic space.

Designing a 3 year vision and a One Year Strategic Sprint all sit in the strategic space, as do understanding and communicating your 'purpose'.

The strategic thinking and actions drive the business direction and feed the machine which is *operations* and *support.*

An example would be forming a partnership with a company that can introduce you to a 100s of clients a year. This would be a smart strategic move and would feed the operations and need support. Without it, there maybe no business going through operations to be supported.

I worked with a client where they hadn't quite understood how important it was to think strategically. That was until one day, three months after we discussed it, the MD did a business deal, on the golf course, that earned him his whole year's salary in one hour. Now he understands the importance and he gets to play golf and meet the right people too.

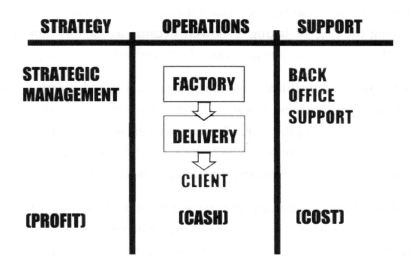

Now back to your list:

If you now look at your list, you'll see that you've got a whole bunch of things.- How many of them are Operations, how many are Support and how many are Strategic?

This will tell you where you are spending your time. Now if you've got lots of support on your list, ask yourself: is this good use of your time? Unless that's your skillset, outsource it! If you do, you'll have more time for Operations and Strategy.

When I do this exercise with a room full of business owners I ask them how much time they think owners of businesses spend doing strategy. Unsurprisingly, the answer is usually less than 5% and by their own admission they say that's usually at the weekend, or when walking the dog, or taking a shower. Because as soon as they walk into their businesses they get dragged into operations and support.

So I want you to think how much time you spend creating joint ventures, partnerships, looking at your positioning and doing the things to generating P.R.O.F.I.T.S. in a strategic way. That time spent doing the strategic work is where the P.R.O.F.I.T.S. are generated in business. It then passes to operations and is backed up by support.

Look at where you spend your time and if you look at your list you'll see where you spend your time and my challenge to you is that for the next 48 hours, every piece of paper you touch, every phone call you make or receive, every conversation you're involved in, ask yourself is it support, operations or strategic? Now you'll begin to see where you're spending your time.

To give you one more example of this, just imagine that we're having a meeting about growing our business and we're all arriving at our offices but the receptionist is particularly rude on this day before we walk into the meeting. So what's the first conversation we're going to have? It's going to be about that receptionist. If you apply this concept to the meeting which is on growth (strategy) it's clear that the rudeness of the receptionist is a HR issue to be dealt with in a Support meeting, and that's for another day and gets referred to an HR meeting.

We're in the meeting to talk about strategic management and growth and it's not about the receptionist so you get very clear about how you spend your time. I recommend blocking out time in your diary for these functions. An example of this is my financial adviser who has strategy days where he doesn't see his clients. Operational days where he meets his client – usually 5 a day, and days where he is prospecting new clients.

If you call on a strategy day you won't get to speak with him, but you will go in the diary for a call back or meeting on an operations day. All his admin is done by his PA, including running his diary. The SOS model below is an example of a functioning business SOS:

The Functional Business		
Business Strategy	**Business Operations**	**Business Support**
Business planning & management	Operations Management	Accounting & finance
Client management services	Training	Human resources
Distribution	Marketing	Information technology
Joint Ventures	Sales	Compliance

	Product Design	Legal
	Product Delivery	Secretarial
	Client Services	Administration
		Premise management

All the things on the business support list you can outsource straight away to free you up. Now if you look at the business operations: yes you can probably do all these, but is it best use of your time?

If you make a bit more time for business strategy instead, where might your business be? It could be you doing that deal on the golf course rather than being stuck in operations and missing that opportunity and golf day altogether.

I hope you're getting a sense of this now and if you do this well then you can start to look at how your PROFITS will flow as a result of it.

Skills for Business	JAN	FEB	MAR	APR	MAY	JUN	JUL	AUG
Working Days	22	20	22	21	23	21	22	23
Other Business	0	0	0	0	0	0	0	0
Holidays/Family	4	4	4	4	4	5	4	8
Team Days	0	0	0	0	0	0	0	0
Training	1	1	1	1	1	1	1	1
Planning	4	2	2	1	1	1	1	1
Workshops & Conferences	0	0	0	0	0	0	0	0
Client days	5	5	12	12	12	12	12	12
Total Days Out	14	12	19	18	18	19	18	22
Available Days	8	8	3	3	5	2	4	1
Actual Days Charged	5	5	12	12	12	12	12	12

Here is an example of how I started out planning my time, looking at a 6 month period from January – August.

First thing to recognise is that a month may have 28,29,30 or 31 days in it, but if you take out the weekends immediately you have reduced time available. In my example, January has 22 working days.

Now you can see I've further divided those days into things I need to get done during the month like holidays, training, planning and existing client visits.

In this example in January I only have 8 days available because the business and holidays have claimed 14 days. Of those 14 days only 5 are chargeable.

Now if we move to August it can be seen that my capacity is really being challenged. Yes I've planned my time but you can quickly see that I only have one spare day – best not be sick then.

From this I am able to work out that I can see only 12 clients per month. I'll therefore, need to earn sufficient to run my business and support my lifestyle from those twelve days, as on the other days I will be running my business. I've reached my pinch point.

To increase my capacity I've got to either take more staff on, outsource some work, or change the way I do business. I opted for a one to many approach. What if I could get all my clients to see me together on one day? Now, I can increase my capacity.

The other thing to bear in mind is that I probably won't always run at full capacity, so I created a set point of 7 clients a month as a break even/profit.

What I realised was that I needed to earn my money from 6-8 client days per month. Knowing this allowed me too take what I need to earn for the year, divided it by 10 (not 12) and that gave me how much I need to earn in a month and that tells me how much I need to earn each day I'm out in the field delivering to run my business.

I divided by ten months not twelve as I figured I'd be on holiday, or clients would be in December and August, or there would be cancellations along the way. The margin for error, if you will.

The other thing to bear in mind is that there are market forces. Will the market forces tolerate that? I need to consider that as well. It gives me an indication of how much I need to earn each day I'm in front of a client and it gives me a day rate or a retainer. I tend to work on retainers. This way I can cash flow my business over the year.

Skills for
Business

Revenue

Client	# Days	JAN	FEB	MAR	APR	MAY	JUN	JUL	AUG	SEP	OCT	NOV	DEC	Totals
Client 1	1	1500	1500	1500	1500	1500	1500	1500	1500	1500	1500	1500	1500	18,,000
Client 2	1	1500	1500	1500	1500	1500	1500	1500	1500	1500	1500	1500	1500	18,,000
Client 3	1	1500	1500	1500	1500	1500	1500	1500	1500	1500	1500	1500	1500	18,,000
Client 4	1	1500	1500	1500	1500	1500	1500	1500	1500	1500	1500	1500	1500	18,,000
Client 5	1		1500	1500	1500	1500	1500	1500	1500	1500	1500	1500	1500	16,,500

By knowing what I need to earn each month, I was able to set my day rate.

I started in January with 4 clients, in this projected example. I knew that I was going to put them on a retainer. A retainer for me meant an annual fee divided by twelve monthly payments. This allowed me to do 10 days delivery over the year with 2 days for background working when they were on holiday.

So I have 4 clients here in January, I have 5 by December. In reality, I've been able to build this a lot higher than this; this is just a forecast. By now it's looking more like 8 or 9 clients. But using this method, I could see what my annual income was going to be and I could see what my monthly income was going to be too.

This enabled me to manage my business accordingly and use the revenue wisely in my business. If a client drops off, I can slot another in.

You can do this exercise for yourself and others in your business too.

Capacity Mapping

Let's move on to *process* now and map your key processes so they can be easily replicated and reviewed as you grow. Before I get into the meat of this section, I should tell you about the time where I learned the hard way about processes. I was a student, listening to somebody teaching me about processes; as a group we were asked to write a process for opening a box of matches. When we'd written our process, we had to read it out loud so our tutor could follow the process.

What happened next was quite humorous. I read out my process which was:

1. pick up the box of matches,

2. push the centre through to reveal the matches.

I never got to step three, because all the matches fell on the floor.

Why? Because I had not identified that the matchbox needed to be face up.

Writing process isn't as straight forward as it seems.You've got to treat it step by step and always make it "idiot proof". I was the idiot in the example, because I hadn't said turn the box face up. So when you're writing process, make sure you think about it in the most simplistic terms, as if you were teaching it to the most simple person. Make it simple and easy to follow. Make it straightforward.

When I'm presenting to clients I use a very simple example to emphasise the point regarding systems being of importance and I thought I'd share it with you. In the diagram below I ask my clients to circle and join the numbers up from 1 to 52. I'm going to ask you to do the same.

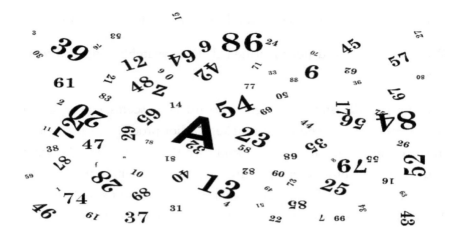

How did you get on. If you followed the process you'll have struggled to get any further than 5. Why is that? Because some of the processes are hidden, obscured or in business simply inefficient. If we strip away some of the unnecessary obstructions – the A in this case - we can then begin to see the process emerging – number 5.

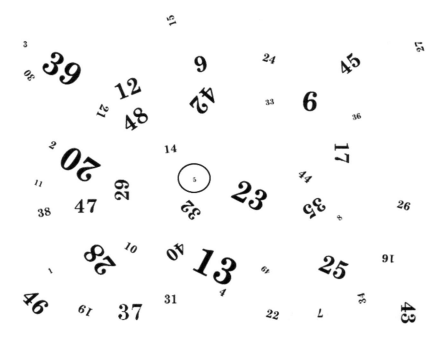

Now we have removed the waste it can be tracked much more easily.

When a client, new member of staff or anyone visits your business without systems and processes they will see diagram 1 – how do they find their way around your business? When you document and identify process it then becomes a lot easier for anyone to see how your business works. Doing this early on in your business will save a lot of heart ache later.

So here's a more practical example of what I'm talking about.

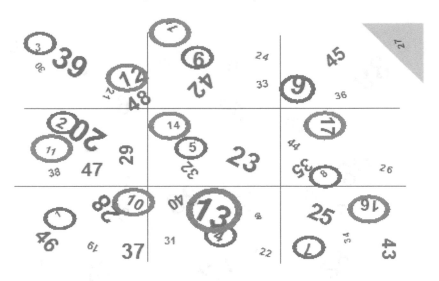

What is a process?

1. Agree objectives
2. Design questionnaire
3. Build target database
4. Call customers
5. Analyse findings
6. Write report

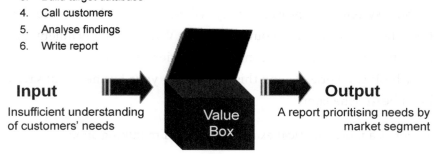

Input
Insufficient understanding of customers' needs

Value Box

Output
A report prioritising needs by market segment

If you're writing process to really understand your customer's needs then it may look a bit like this. If a company had insufficient understanding of their customer needs, they would need to write a process to discover and produce a report prioritising the needs by segment market. Firstly, they'd need to agree the objectives, then they'd have to design the questionnaire and build the target database. Then they'd need to call the customers and analyse the findings and finally write the report. So you can quite quickly see there is a lot of steps that need to happen and that becomes the process which they follow.

As we move forward I'm going to get you to think about selecting processes in your business that you need to look at and then we're going to map them and measure them. Later we are also going to see if there are any faults within them, identify root causes that stop bad things happening. We're going to look at processes that don't work and finally how to remove wastage in process so we can record it.

Let's just start the mapping process as it is.

If you are a business that's growing, then these may be some typical issues you may need processes for.

- Innovative new offerings

- Raising finance

- Building a supplier base

- Recruiting key individuals

- Finding new customers

- Selling to new customers

- Planning production/delivery

- Manufacturing the goods/service

- Purchasing materials

- Training employees

- Delivering product/service

- Building strategic alliances

- Paying suppliers

- Billing customers

- Managing overseas agents

- Managing projects

- Launching new products

- Selling-on to existing customers

But which are absolutely key to your high growth?

Will it be recruiting and training the right staff? Setting the right culture?

All these things that are critical to growth have processes that sit behind them. Working out which ones to prioritise, which ones are most important to you, is critical to ensure you focus on the right processes.

Exercise: defining your key business processes

Step 1) What do your key customers tell you?

- What are the processes that drive your uniqueness in the market?
- What processes does your organisation need to focus on?
- What are your main offerings?
- What are the processes that produce each?

Write down some key processes from your customers' view

This enables you to understand the key process your customers go through when buying and the process that you need to match and document.

Exercise: defining your key business processes

Step 2) Which processes are critical to successfully achieving your Vision Maximiser & 1 year Sprint plan?

- Which processes cost the most in terms of time and money?
- Which processes will help you compete in the future?
- Which processes have your most successful high growth competitors got right?
- Which processes are the most difficult to scale rapidly or replicate easily?

Write down some key processes critical to your growth

One of the difficulties I see quite often when attempting to rapidly replicate is that the business owner has all the knowledge in their head and it is not documented anywhere. If they are the main sales person, what happens when they are ill? or when they can only do so many appointments? They become the pinch point in the business. Therefore, to grow, it is necessary to unpick this knowledge, document it, and teach it to others in the business. This is even more critical as business owners reach retirement, as the knowledge will be lost to the business forever if not captured.

The challenge is: how do we get it out of their head? How do we put it into a process? How do we teach it to others? The best way I have seen is to have a process person shadow and capture the information, rather than having the business leader / expert try to write it down.

Often, these experts do things intuitively, like second nature, and it is much easier for an external person to observe their processes than it is for the expert themselves to articulate it. Alternatively, have sales people go with the expert and have them capture the information; challenging and learning from the expert as they go.

Exercise: defining your key business processes

Step 3) Rate each process using these questions:

- How critical is this process to your organisation's sprint plan and vision maximiser success?
- How critical is the process to attracting new customers an retaining existing ones?
- How critical is this process to rapidly replicating, so that the 1,000th "unit" runs as smoothly as the 1st

To make this exercise easier, I'm going to ask you to identify some key processes critical to your business. Then, we are going to run some filters over them. But first let me give you an example: in this case, a burger franchise.

Key business process evaluation grid

Rate between 0 "not at all" through to 10 "especially critical"

Processes under consideration	How critical is the process to the successful implementation of your sprint plan / vision maximiser?	How critical is the process to attracting new customers and retaining existing ones?	How critical is this process to "rapidly replicating", so that the 1,000th "unit" runs as smoothly as the 1st?	Total
Attracting high quality Franchisees	4	8	10	22
Securing supplier of frozen fries	2	3	9	14
Local customer attraction campaigns	7	10	10	27
Innovating new meal offerings	3	5	3	11
Recruitment of Counter Staff	3	7	9	19
Preparation of burger pattis	4	8	10	22
Adherence to food cleanliness rules	9	7	10	26
Frying the burgers	8	9	10	27

You can see from this example the franchise have identified what they consider key processes to their growth. However, once they ran key filters over these processes it became evident that some processes they thought were critical to growth actually were not. For example, "innovative new meal offerings", when considered through the three prisms of achieving the one year sprint goal, gaining new customers, and replicating, is actually far less important than any of the other objectives. Innovative meals is not critical to creating this franchise's success.

Now it is your turn. Pick some key processes that you consider are critical to your growth and run the filters over them. Rate between 0 – "not at all" and 10 – "especially critical"

Key business process evaluation grid

Rate between 0 "not at all" through to 10 "especially critical"

Processes under consideration	How critical is the process to the successful implementation of your sprint plan / vision maximiser?	How critical is the process to attracting new customers and retaining existing ones?	How critical is this process to "rapidly replicating", so that the 1,000th "unit" runs as smoothly as the 1st?	Total

Did you find some red herrings or things you shouldn't be doing? This exercise ensures that you are focusing on the key processes to your success.

To do this well, you need what I call a "process for process". We have now selected our key processes and evaluated them, which is step 1. The next step in the process is to map them out.

Key steps to improving a process

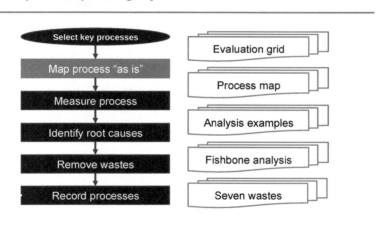

In this step we are going to map out a process, or more accurately, I'm going to ask you to design one. To give you an idea, here is an example of a simple guide / process map I designed for a Motivational Appraisal Process that I sell to companies. You can use this format or you can use what is called a 'swim lane' format.

For the 'swim lane', I've used an example of a workshop I was commissioned to run for a client.

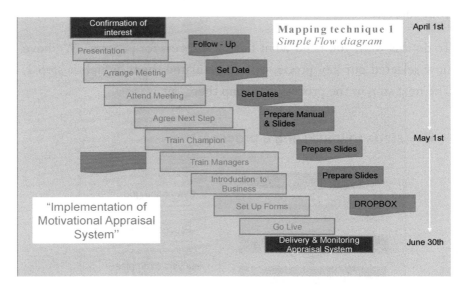

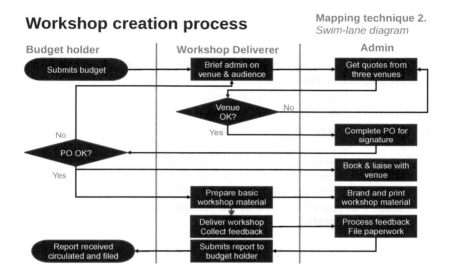

I want you to take a process, maybe one you identified earlier or one that is not working so well, and map it out as it is.

Do this in landscape on the biggest sheet of paper you can find and I would recommend using post-it notes.

Exercise: process mapping

- Map out one of your own "as is" key business processes using either **flow diagram** or **swim lane**
- Good and bad bits – **not as you want it to look**
- Start with naming the process
- Write the output at the bottom of the sheet and the start (or input) at the top of the page
- Complete the tasks that turn the input into the output
- Describe the current tasks in a clear, succinct, high level manner. Use of active verb / noun (e.g. "drill hole") rather than long sentences
- Discuss with your partner and ask for feedback on how your process map could be clearer

I encourage staff to get involved in designing processes like this because if they design it they buy into it and they adhere to it. If you design it and impose it, they probably won't like it and they probably won't adhere to it. Get their 'buy in' and they'll take ownership to follow it and improve it and it will save you a lot of time and energy.

Now the question once you've done this is: "does the flow chart truly represent the day-to-day reality in both tasks and sequence?"

If you're genuinely looking to improve it, have you avoided the temptation to map it as it should happen rather than how it actually happens?

My experience around a process like this is that quite often there isn't an existing flow chart so people tend to write it as they'd like it to be.

What I also find is that people are not used to doing these flow charts, which is why I encourage them to use Post-It notes, because they will find they are moving things about or missing vital stages out, resulting in a necessary re-jig. Once you've re-jigged it and sorted it out, then you're in a position to actually agree it.

Have all team members been involved in the process and contributed their knowledge? It is so important for teams to do this because they are at the coal face, they know what's going on. They are the best people to contribute to the process and show you the best way to do it.

If it is a customer-facing process then get your customers involved. Get your customers who are brave enough to look at it and tell you what would really help them. Even the biggest companies with the brightest brains behind them must listen to customers. A very recent example of this is Ubisoft Montreal, a video-game company with a net income of €561 million and one of the most successful in the world, who, at their 2018 E3 convention, revealed their key strategy for improving their games was "the old fashioned way". In other words: to invite their players / customers to the studio, play their games, and give them feedback face to face on their products. That's invaluable information.

A quick recap now:

Your role
[as the one who has to work on the business not in it]

- Does the flowchart truly represent the day to day reality in both tasks and sequence?
- If you're genuinely looking to improve it, have you avoided the temptation to map how it "should" happen rather than how it actually happens?
- Have the team members involved in the process contributed their knowledge?
- Ask internal and /or external customers to provide process improvement objectives / opportunities for improvement

Now we can move to the next step.

Key steps to improving a process

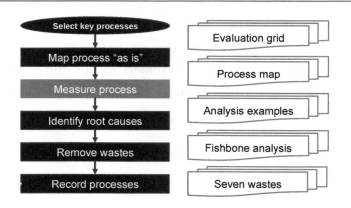

Measure The Process

How do we collect baseline data? How do we put measures against what we've now created in a flow chart? We've mapped it, but now we're going to *measure* it.

There are a several very true sayings that apply here:

"What gets measured gets done"

"There's no quality without measurement"

"You cannot measure what's invisible"

Here are some measurement filters to run over what you have mapped out:

Collect data at points in the process that will help us improve it

Effectiveness	Is it delivering the results we wanted it to against a target? Is it doing the right things?
Efficiency	Is it delivering the results we wanted without wasted time or effort? Is it doing the right things right first time?
Adaptability	Is it producing the results in a way that will flex and scale?

So let's look at a simple example.

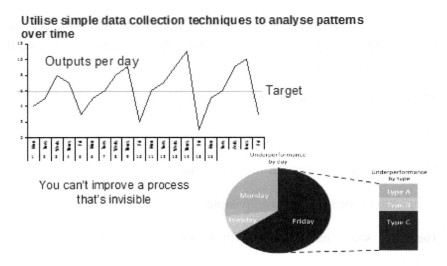

Here's a car manufacturer. Just looking at the output per day you'll notice from this diagram that every Friday there's a dip in performance. The weekend's looming and there's poor performance as a result. Only by measuring it was this organization able to identify that.

Would you buy a car from this company that was made on a Friday? Probably not. This demonstrates the importance of putting measures onto everything that you do.

The next example comes from a telesales campaign.

Three bar analysis - telemarketing campaign that costs £40,000

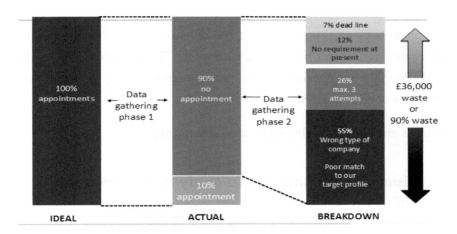

Now if you look at this telemarketing campaign you can see that it has failed spectacularly.

They wanted 100% appointments.

They collected the data, so they had a process for that which is a plus.

But 90% of the appointments they were attempting to contact led to no appointments. 10% of 100% were actual appointments.

7% of the calls were to dead lines.

12% not requirement at present – the wrong client

26% a maximum of 3 attempts to get through

55% were the wrong type of company and a poor match to the target profile.

It comes back to the positioning we did earlier but also shows that this campaign wasn't well thought through. They wasted time, effort and £36,000 on a poorly thought out strategy resulting in 90% waste. In terms of effectiveness, it simply wasn't!

Here is another example using value streaming.

Value stream mapping to analyse how well the process flows

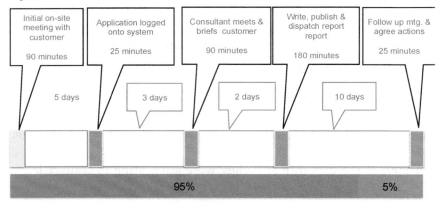

Initial on-site meeting with the customers of 90 minutes.

ACTUAL: 5 Days

Applications logged onto the system is another 25 minutes.

ACTUAL: 3 Days

Consultant meets and briefs the customer takes another 90 minutes. ACTUAL: 2 days

Write, publish and dispatch the report takes another 180 minutes.

ACTUAL: 10 days

Follow up meeting and agreeing the actions adds another 25 minutes.

In reality the process should take just under 7 hours and yet it was taking this business 20 days. Totally inefficient.

Now let's ask another question:

If Amazon were to operate like this, or Apple, how long would they be in business?

The cruel thing about business today is we're all measured by Apple and Amazon's standards. It doesn't matter what business you're in, it's all about speed to market, it's all about efficiency.

If your company is performing anywhere near to this example or your processes are anything like this then you can just see who's going to get the business and who's not.

This company is 95% inefficient and 5% efficient so how long will they stay in business?

Now go back to your process charts and start to put some time frames around how quickly you can deliver.

Exercise: measuring the process ... *to collect baseline data*

- Consider the key business process you mapped earlier

- Annotate the process flow chart with measurement points to asses this process for effectiveness & efficiency

- What format would you want data to be presented in

- Who would make decisions based on the data

In my previous example, there are measure points to make sure the event happens in a timely fashion.

Workshop creation process

Mapping technique 2.
Swim-lane diagram

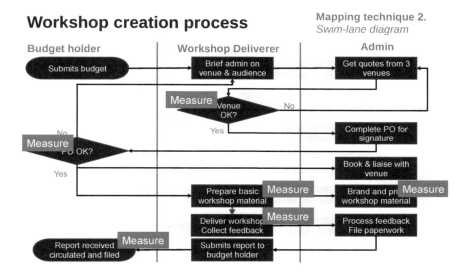

Spend five minutes looking at ways you could refine and find some good short cuts, quick wins, and better ways of serving your client.

The next step in the process is to identify what may be causing inefficiencies in your process – the route cause.

Key steps to improving a process

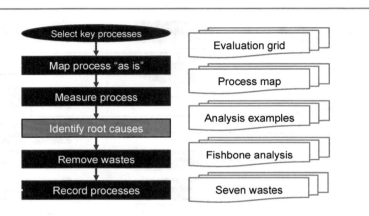

Identify Root Causes

Now we're going to look at improving the process by understanding the root cause and stripping out waste so let's deal with the root cause first.

What causes variations in processes? It can be a number of things:

What normally causes a process to vary?

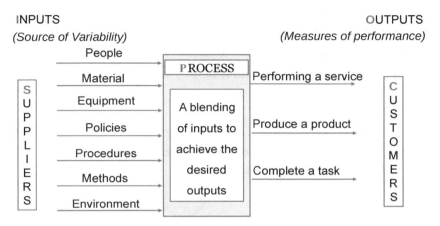

As you can see from the diagram it could be your:

- People – are the following process?

- Equipment – is it up to the task or outdated?

- Policies – are they holding you back from serving your client?

- Procedures – are they out of date? Do they need updating/refining?

- Methods – are you using old methodology when new is available?

- Environment – is it too hot/cold, too cramped etc?

It could be any number of these inputs are not serving you. To get to the bottom of finding out where the inefficiencies occur, there is an exercise I use that enables you to identify where the fault lies. It is called the *fishbone diagram* and it helps you understand root causes.

So here's an example.

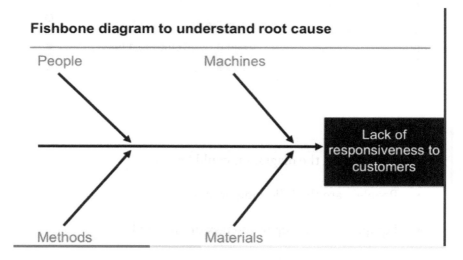

In this example I have put 'lack of responsiveness to customers' as the problem and this goes at the box available at the head of the fish.

Now we can get to the root cause of the problem by working back to that route cause.

To do this you can populate the fish scales with potential input titles.

In this example we are using: People; Methods; Machines; and Materials. However, you can use other titles from the example earlier.

It could be *people*, it could be *machines*, it could be *methods* or it could be *materials*. Feel free to include other options not listed. Put the problem in the 'head' of the fish and work backwards to see where the problem(s) lie. So let's give you an example.

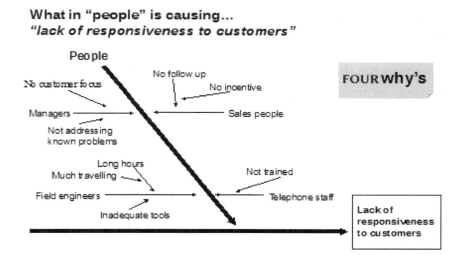

So in this example, lack of responsiveness to customers, if we just look at the *people* aspect it could be that:

- the managers have no customer focus and the managers are not addressing known problems

- the sales people have no incentive, therefore there's no desire to follow up

- the telephone staff are simply not trained

- the field engineers are travelling too much, working too long and don't have the right equipment

In this simple example it could be that the people are at fault or it could be a deeper issue that there are no systems for the staff to follow. Either way we have found the fault(s).

If we then run this process on all areas of the diagram, the scale of the problem becomes even clearer.

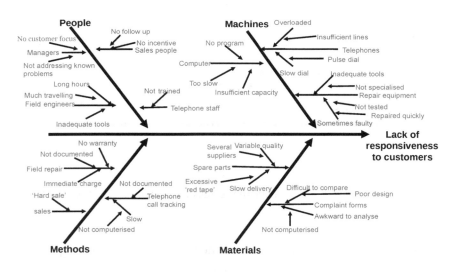

If you look deeper, it can be seen that:

- in the field repair, there's no documentation and no warranties

- the sales are too hard – hard selling

- in the telephone call tracking there's no documentation, it's slow and not computerised

If you start to look at materials, you get the same sort of picture.

- poor design, difficult to compare, awkward to analyse, not computerised – and that's just the complaints

- in spare parts, they're of variable quality, excessive, lots of red tape, slow delivery

In this example we can really track the issue back to route cause(s).

Imagine you get a team to work on this to identify what's not working and why it's not working. You can strip back to the basics, and you can very quickly start to change things in your business to reduce these blockages to make things flow much better.

What I would recommend is that you engage in a root cause exercise with your teams or with yourself if you're a single operator working on your own.

Work with the key business processes you mapped earlier for your own business. Write down the main problems or opportunities for improvement in the fish head and choose one scale to start with. Ask the question: "What is it in that is causing the problem to happen?"

Using the *4 whys* technique is a simple way to start.

If someone was late for work, you'd ask:

- **Why are you late for work?**

    o   I missed the bus.

- **Why** did you miss the bus?

    o   Because I got up late.

- **Why** did you get up late?

    o   Because I stayed up until midnight.

- **Why** did you stay up until midnight?

So, with four questions you can quite quickly get to the root cause of why that person was late. Actually, the problem is nothing to do with bus timetabling, but their own approach to their working day. The solution is clear: go to bed earlier, get up earlier, get on an earlier bus. This is a very simple example, but it reflects the process of trying to fine tune what you do so that you are quick, efficient and effective.

Now it's your turn:

Exercise: determining the root cause of your key business process's problem

- Work with the key business process you mapped earlier for your own business

- Write down the main problem or opportunity for improvement in the fish head

- Choose one "bone" asking "what is it in … that is causing the problem to happen?"

- Use "four Whys" technique to drill down to root cause

Fishbone diagram to understand root cause

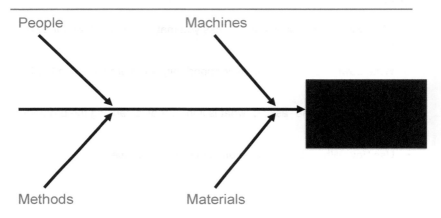

The Seven Internal Service Wastes

Key steps to improving a process

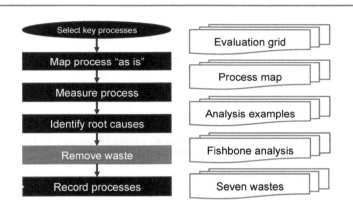

In this section we're going to look at the seven internal service wastes that can occur in your business.

If I visited your business and put on my "waste goggles" what sort of things would I see happening (or not happening) in your key business processes that would suggest waste or non-value added activity?

If I walked around what would I see, where would the inefficiencies be, what would be happening in your organization?

I'm going to use recruitment as an example, because everyone at some level is familiar with recruitment processes.

In my experience most businesses recruit too fast and fire too slow and as a result end up with poor staff. Really they should take time with their recruitment. It's the reverse of the norm: recruit slow and fire fast. There's a lot that could be said on this issue, but I think that's for another book! For now, let's look at the process broadly to help us understand internal service wastes.

Here are the seven wastes with examples of each type of waste:

1) Unnecessary delay

On the part of customers (internal or external) waiting for service, for delivery or in a queue. Anything not arriving when anticipated/promised.

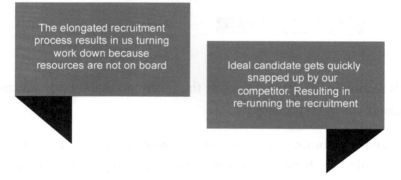

2) Wasted effort

Activities that don't return sufficient value, possibly a "sledge hammer to crack a nut" or simple duplication.

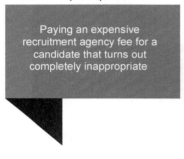

3) Unnecessary movement

Excessive travel or transportation, lack of a one stop shop or even poor ergonomics.

4) Unclear communication

Unclear communication and the wastes of seeking clarification and confusion that arises

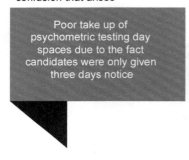

5) Incorrect inventory

Activities that result because something (or someone) is not available. Alternatively too much unnecessary resource/product stored "just in case".

6) Opportunity lost

Opportunities lost to gain, retain or win something

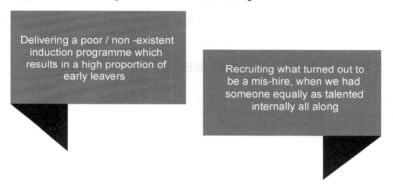

7) Errors

Additional activities which were needed to rectify mistakes, plus any defective outputs that were generated

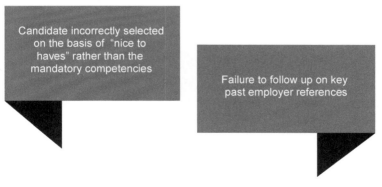

I think the wastes are pretty self explanatory. Now I want you to focus on your business and think where wastes may be occurring for you.

To help you I've designed an exercise and a grid for you to work with:

Exercise: Seven service wastes

Working with the key business process you mapped earlier for your own business, write down on Post-It notes examples of things that I would see happening or not happening if I visited your businesses with my "Waste Goggles" on in relation to this specific process

- Try and generate a number of examples for each of the seven types of waste as they occur currently in your process
- Think about what stops the process from flowing as well as what goes wrong
- Work in a group to individually share and present and map these onto the A0 sheet

Your seven internal service wastes

1. Delay - Waiting for service, for delivery or in a queue. Anything not arriving when anticipated.	**2. Wasted Effort** - Activities that don't return sufficient value, possibly a "sledge hammer to crack a nut" or duplication.
3. Unnecessary Movement - Too much excessive travel, lack of a one stop shop or even poor ergonomics.	**4. Unclear Communication** - Unclear communication and the wastes associated with confusion that arises.
5. Incorrect Inventory - Something is not available or too much is available like unnecessary inventory	**6. Opportunity Lost** - Opportunities lost to gain, retain or win something
7. Errors - Rectifying mistakes plus any defective outputs that were generated	

So, based on what we now know about the root causes of any problems, the opportunities to improve, plus the wastes that need to be stripped out, here are some questions for you.

- What steps in the process need to be changed? You've had a good look at the process now. What steps would you change?

- What specific new ideas should be implemented so there could be better ways of doing things?

- How are you going to implement them?

- How are you going to improve?

- Are there any risks associated with the proposed changes?

- What will the change to the process cost?

- Is it going to be costly? E.G. Do you need to updated IT or do you need new machinery?

- Who is responsible for implementing the change?

- Who is going to take ownership to ensure it happens and that there accountability?

- What has to be done to implement the change?

- What actions need to be taken?

- Have you identified them clearly?

- How will the implementation be controlled?

- Who's going to take ownership again and take control to make sure it happens?

Record Processes

Key steps to improving a process

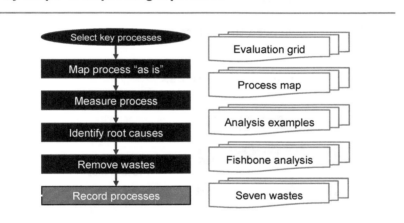

The final part of this is to record and improve the process. Continually improve, capture and publish in an operations manual so when you do this you need to record it.

Recording the process is really important. The secret is to make the process foolproof so that it can be delivered by people with the lowest level of skill. This is the theory. Personally, I prefer great people running great process, as I believe it produces the best results.

To help you think about this more clearly consider the following:

How would you write a process for a five year old to bake some cakes? It's as simple as that – if you reduce the number of ingredients to a minimum (use sub-assemblies), reduce the number of steps to minimize it, show what the finished product (output) looks like maybe using photographs. All of this is going to simplify it so that staff and clients can grab it and understand it.

So here's what we've been through so far:

Key steps to improving a process

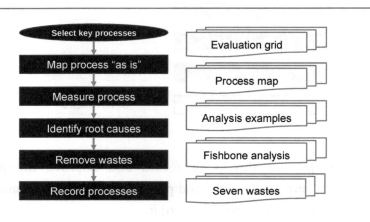

First of all we talked about process and why process is important. Then we selected a key process and used an evaluation grid to make sure you're not wasting time on processes that are probably not important for growth. We mapped it 'as it is' with flow charts and swim lanes in order to see the situation *now*. We then put some measures on it to frame the efficiencies and effectiveness of the process. We looked at processes that currently aren't working correctly to identified the root cause. We used the fish diagram and the *four whys*. We looked at the seven wastes – how you remove wasteful processes and elements in your business. We used the example of recruitment to demonstrate waste. And then of course it's about recording the process to make sure it's agreed and documented in the manuals for staff to follow it.

Remember, in all of this: The best way to get staff to follow is to get them to be involved in the design of the process or the improvement of the process. Beyond this, they might also see something you can't!

So what I've tried to achieve in this part is:

- Growth with fewer problems

- Turnover at ever reducing marginal cost

- Output from less expensive people. Although I say less expensive people, you just want great systems that great people can run

- Leaner processes with less waste

- Success for the business with less reliance on you for your business should you decide to move on and sell.

- If it's robust and if the system and processes work then when you come to sell your business you don't need to be involved.

- You can be working "on" your business not "in" it and that's the key to being free to generating revenue and profits.

So what are you going to start doing, stop doing, do more of and do less of as a result of looking at process?

7. SERVE YOUR CLIENTS

It is no longer just a case of delivering a service. These days there is an expectation that the service will be *exceptional*. As I mentioned earlier, all businesses are now judged against Amazon and Apple's standards.

If you want your clients to refer you all over town then this is critical. These are becoming the accepted norm. However, interestingly, these major companies service their clients differently, but both have exceptional service levels.

What are your service levels like? A word of warning here: Be very clear what your service levels are and are not. This is critical because it's easy to exceed expectation when you have just a few clients and capacity in your business to over service. But what happens when those few clients become many? Will you be able to maintain it? If not, your service levels will fall and your business may suffer.

A simple but practical example I see all too often in start up businesses is newsletters. When the business starts the business owner produces a monthly newsletter. Then, as they become busier, there is less time to create this newsletter and a few months go by before the next newsletter.

It is therefore imperative that you are clear what is a standard – what the client can expect by default – and what is an extra – something that you do for them that is a one off.

Let me give you an example. Here's an exercise I've done with numerous clients large and small. I ask them a very simple question: What do you do to raise the level of your clients' energy around you as a business?

Depending on the size of the organization, I'll get different responses.

Let's take a medium sized accountancy firm I coach. This is what they do:

- Newsletters

- One to one strategy meetings

- Local networking events for the community

- Directors Forum Events

- Golf Days

- Charity Events

Now, as they have become busier, the local networking event has become a bit of a millstone around their neck as it takes a lot of resources to organize. However, if they don't do it they will create a negative impact on those who regularly attend. They therefore are committed to putting on these events in the knowledge that they are *not* going to raise clients' energy; it is now an *expected* service, a norm, a standard. Stopping it will cause a negative impact, but keeping it going is merely 'business as usual'.

It's the same with the golf day. What do the attendees say on leaving? "See you next year". Now, they are expected to run it again and again, forever, creating a standard.

I was with one client who spent £70,000 a year to raise client energy around their business. However, when we ran this filter over the activates, they had all become standards that did not raise the energy of the client. This client is now 'committed' to spending £70k on standard expectations regardless.

Funnily enough, it is the same with staff. If I ask business owners what they do to raise the energy of their staff they will say we:

- Pay Them

- Give them Bonuses

- Holidays

- Duvet days

- Private health insurance

- Christmas parties

Now, if we ignore the obvious error of thought that 'paying staff' is what should keep them motivated (never mind how we treat them, whether the work is stimulating, etc) and look at the other elements, we can see that many things that are perhaps intended as a one off special events or treats become part of employee expectation. I know many companies that have had to either cancel or scale down their Christmas party due to a tough financial year. The effect on staff morale is devastating. Yet, really, the extravagant Christmas party last year was only meant as a one off celebration for a particularly good year. The last thing you want is to create negative energy. So again, these standards need to be managed.

What I'm saying here: it's possible to delight your clients so they come back for more and refer you all over town without getting caught in a standards trap.

This doesn't mean you can't do any of the things listed so far. By all means do some or all of them, but be aware they become standards fast and are therefore considered as expected services which don't raise energy.

Consider setting events up that are extras never to be repeated. This is exclusive, which in and of itself creates excitement. The key is to stress that these activities are 'one' offs never to be repeated.

Here are some examples:

- A 50th Birthday Party celebration (for the company or perhaps even for a senior person within the company)

- A one off celebration to mark a good financial year, and thank clients (or staff) for their hard work

- Or even more creatively: We know you love Football and

218

we've been lucky enough to acquire some world cup tickets. It's unlikely we'll ever get them again but we thought of you.

Now you've freed up your £70K budget to really raise the energy of your clients without any future expectation being set. This means each year you can choose how to use your £70k to raise energy.

The point I'm making here is that it is really important to serve your client well so they buy the next product/service off you and refer you all over town, without falling into the trap of creating loads of burdensome standards.

You might like to look at the diagram below and run what you are doing against it.

Let's take the golf day as an example:

If you don't run it next year it becomes a negative.

If you do run it then it becomes a neutral not raising energy at all.

Now let's take running an extra:

We've had an exceptional year so for this year only we're running a special client day which you are invited to. It is unlikely to happen again.

Now you are delivering an extra, something special, which will not happen again. In the diagram below it raises energy if done. If you don't do it no one was any the wiser so it is neutral.

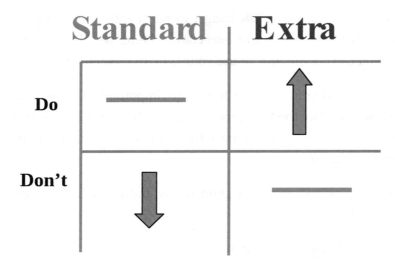

In conclusion: REMEMBER TO SERVE YOUR CLIENT BUT DO IT IN THE RIGHT WAY so they buy more and refer you. Also remember that: BUSINESS GOES WHERE IT'S INVITED AND LOOKED AFTER!

Turning on Your Profits Tap | Steve Jones

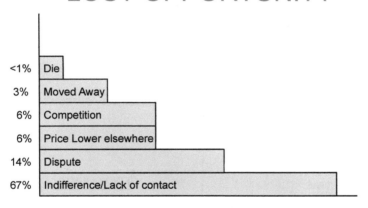

Business Goes where it is invited!!

© Copyright 2009 Steve Jones

The Assessment – The Acid Test

Turning on YOUR P.R.O.F.I.T.S. Wheel
Where are you NOW?

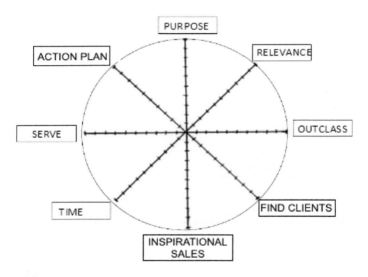

Scoring: Add all 8 scores, divide by 8, x 10 to get percentage score
80+: You are on course for success
60-79: You have many elements in place, tweaking needed.
35-59: Some big changes are needed
0-34: Urgent Action is needed
Get Your ACTION Plan: Contact Steve Jones on 07971 882628 (m)
Email: steve@skillsforbusinesstraining.co.uk
Web: www.skillsforbusinesstraining.co.uk

Before you consign this book to history – which is what I have done with many a book in my time, please take time to assess yourself against the P.R.O.F.I.T.S. Wheel. This is the last insight in this book, and I hope it becomes a default check you can do for yourself.

What I'd like you to do now is to take the 'acid test' by scoring yourself against this wheel to see where you are.

You may remember in the opening introduction I asked you to score a tick, a cross, or a neutral against the contextual diagram to P.R.O.F.I.T.S. to see where blockages may occur. We are going a step further here as I challenge you to actually score each stage out of 10 on the WHEEL of P.R.O.F.I.T.S.

0 = Not at all

10= It's 100% Happening

and if it's neither give it a score out of 10.

Here are some questions to help you score accurately:

- PURPOSE: Do you have a compelling 3 year vision and one year sprint breakthrough and is it totally communicated throughout the business?

- RELEVANCE: Is your product what people want and need and is it future proofed (will it be required in years to come or be redundant).

- OUTCLASS THE CROWD: Do you have a clear market position? Do customers know what you do, how you do it, what price you charge, and service you deliver?

- FIND CLIENTS: Do you have a clear process for building relationships with strategic partners who will send you clients? Does it work every time. Do you get pre sold business as a result?

- INSPIRATIONAL SALES: Do you have an inspirational sales process with integrity that focuses on the customers needs? Do you close your sales meetings with a client on board often, seldom, never?

- TIME: Are you totally effective and efficient in all that you do. Do you have systems and processes in place? Do they work for you? Do you manage your capacity well?

- SERVE: Do you clients love you to bits and buy repeat or more services and do they rave about you and refer you all over town?

- ACTION PLAN: Do you have an ACTION PLAN to create the perfect P.R.O.F.I.T.S. Wheel?

Once you've completed the diagram, please join the dots up with lines.

Now look at your wheel. If that were a wheel going down the road, how would it be going? This is a representation of your ability to generate revenue and profits right now.

If you have a perfect wheel great – the job's done. If not, you can now see clearly where you need to put your focus.

I have added in an additional step called the ACTION PLAN as it will be necessary to address any areas where a perfect 10 was not scored. You can now go back to the relevant chapters to assess what to do. However, before you do that, here is another neat tool to create that action plan.

ACTION PLAN:

Using a well known coaching methodology called the GROW Model it is possible to agree an action plan.

Let's assume that we scored low on PURPOSE and we want to get to a perfect 10.

We would use the GROW model like this:

Goal: The questions you ask here establish the steps (short-medium and long-term goal) that need to be taken.

EXAMPLE GOAL: To have a clear vision and one year plan in place for the business by Friday 28th September 2018.

Reality: This step is about exploring the *current situation*. Sometimes this will give you an opportunity to explore the obstacles you are facing. At the very least it allows you to become clear about any problems you may face in achieving the goal. There is a saying in coaching: 'The reason you can't have what you want in life is the story you tell yourself about why you can't have it.'

It is the same here. We are all guilty at times, including me, of telling ourselves stories about why we can't have things.

This section helps identify the obstacles and stories so we can recognise them and no longer use them as an excuse.

EXAMPLE REALITY: Not enough time, too busy, people know what we do we don't need a plan, I won't get buy in, we don't have the funds, we are fine as we are, plans are for other people not us, can't get the team together etc

Options: This is where we look at the ways to attain the goal and overcome the hurdle/stories. List as many options as possible – I usually ask for 20 things you can do differently, as I want to challenge my clients beyond the half dozen they already have thought of and not acted on. Some options may become apparent that are not feasible, but this is why it is useful to explore all possible ways. It is also a useful way to see where your limiting beliefs are by what options you suggest and the ones you discard – and on what basis.

EXAMPLE OPTION: Find the time, put a team together, hire a coach, put a strategy day aside, get everyone together to discuss the importance of putting a plan together, ask everyone to read the

'Turning on Your P.R.O.F.I.T.S book', buy the book for everyone, clear diary dates, etc

Will: At this stage it is necessary to really drill down to get the detail so it is clear exactly what must be undertaken, how and when. Establish your commitment to carry the plan out. How determined and committed are you/and or your team, e.g. on scale of 1-10 (10 being highly committed)? This is about creating accountability to take action – who will hold you to account?

EXAMPLE WILL:

ACTION 1: We will hire a coach to facilitate our session by Monday 10th September 2018 – commitment level 8 – I will let the team know by email close of play on 10th September who the coach is

ACTION 2: Book a venue for the Strategy Day on Friday 28th September - commitment level 8 – I will let the team know by email close of play on 10th September 2018.

ACTION 3: Send out preparatory documents for the Strategy Day by close of play Friday 14th September 2018 - commitment level 8 – I will send documents by email close of play on 14th September.

In my experience if the commitment level falls below an 8 it won't happen and you'll need to explore the low score and regain commitment.

CONCLUSION

My intention in writing this book was and is to give existing and potential business owners a quick and easy way of strategically thinking about their respective businesses.

It's a given that all businesses need to generate revenue and profit if they are to survive and indeed thrive.

The ingredients of that success can be daunting. Life and business would be so much easier if you just did what you are good at and the money showed up. Unfortunately, there are hundreds of other things a business owner needs to do over and above their passion if they truly wish to succeed in business – all of which they probably didn't sign up for when they set out to follow their passion.

My focus in this book has been to demystify the confusion and bring clarity into being, a way of thinking around your business and what needs to be done to truly turn on your P.R.O.F.I.T.S Tap.

It all starts with your purpose and vision but this on its own is not enough. 'Vision without action is a daydream. Action with vision a nightmare' (a Japanese proverb quote by Richard Alan Krieger in *Civilization's Quotations: Life's Ideal*) – so you need both.

You do need to be relevant and not be providing products and services that are or will become obsolete. Hopefully you now won't fall into this trap. If your market place becomes disruptive it is my wish that you are prepared.

Critical to your business success is that you hold a position in your clients' minds when they think of your product or service. More importantly that needs to be the correct position. I hope you have gained clarity in this area and please if in any doubt head back to the chapter. Equally, ask your clients – they will quickly tell you.

Creating a position is one thing, but you still may be 'the best kept secret', so you need to know how to find clients. If you use the 'supermarket' analogy in this book you can easily feed yourself with clients for the rest of your business life. Remember, do this well and it will literally be '10 phone calls, 10 appointments and 10 sales – oh and they'll be calling you'.

You'll still need to visit these clients though, so you'll need a robust sales process that allows you to convert these potential leads to paying clients. If you've done your positioning well this will be a doddle, but you still need a process. It is my hope that you can now build that process.

Getting a client is one thing, keeping them is another thing. This requires two steps. The first is to manage your personal and businesses time efficiently to allow you to deliver your service in a timely fashion. The biggest challenge today is that of being 'time poor'.

It is my intention to show you how not to fall into that trap by preparing for growth, managing your capacity, and allowing you to exceed client expectation with your delivery.

I truly believe that by following these steps you'll truly turn on your P.R.O.F.I.T.S Tap.

Nothing would give me greater pleasure than to hear that you've used these steps and grown your business and profits.

I wish you all the success in the world...

ABOUT THE AUTHOR

Steve Jones is a well known business coach, public speaker, trainer and consultant. Steve is an expert at creating ideas and strategies that build businesses, drive revenue and improve business position & performance. He has a passion for making companies and their products the best in their product category. He has two upcoming books, co-written with James Sale, the first of which is *Mapping Motivation for Engagement.*

Steve's unique understanding of leadership and management, team building and motivation in business, coupled with his understanding, drive and enthusiasm, clearly set him aside as an expert.

Steve gained his knowledge and expertise firstly by being part of the management team of one of the UK's most phenomenal business success stories.

Steve was part of a management team at Fitness First PLC, which went from a handful of health clubs on the south coast to become the largest independent Health Club Chain in Europe and then the world, taking the AIM and FTSE by storm, all in a seven year period. Steve freely admits: 'one of the keys to our success was putting together robust teams fast and being able to scale our operation!'

Steve followed this by joining International Coaching Giants, Shirlaws International - specialist in SME Coaching – again a company that had an amazing success story, before setting up his company, Skills for Business Training in 2002, where his main focus has been helping businesses and teams strategically grow.

Steve is qualified to the highest level, being a Licentiate Fellow of the Institute of Training and Occupational Learning – a qualification afforded to the few - a master 'train the trainer' in NLP, a master licensee for 'Motivational Maps', Thomas International DISC Profiler, an accredited trainer in 'Performance Coaching' with Newcastle College, and being accredited in 'Leading & Developing High Performance' programmes. Steve also holds the 'Diploma in Management Studies' (DMS) graduating from 'Henley Management College' recently voted in the top ten management colleges in the world.

In 2010 Steve was invited onto the Government's Employee

Engagement Task Force team where he was co-chair and has been contributing his knowledge in the areas of team building, motivation and performance improvement, whilst at the same time running a series of workshops for Grant Thornton's highly acclaimed 'Growth Accelerator Programme'.

Steve took what he learnt about engaged workforces and put his first two companies through his Employee Engagement Programme.

This resulted in both companies subsequently winning awards for demonstrating true growth and innovation with energy and passion for delivering change, whilst demonstrating ambition to develop their workforces to maximize commercial opportunities.

He can be contacted via the below links:

Email: steve@skillsforbusinesstraining.co.uk

Web: www.skillsforbusinesstraining.co.uk

Turning on Your Profits Tap | Steve Jones

Turning on Your Profits Tap | Steve Jones

Turning on Your Profits Tap | Steve Jones

Turning on Your Profits Tap | Steve Jones